full hands full life

THE RADICAL PURSUIT
OF UNWAVERING
JOY IN MOTHERHOOD

MEREDITH JUENGEL

Full Hands, Full Life

Copyright ® 2025 by Meredith Juengel
Published by UNITED HOUSE Publishing
All rights reserved. No portion of this book may be reproduced or shared in any form - electronic, printed, photocopied, recording, or by any information storage or retrieval system, without prior written permission from the publisher. The use of short quotations is permitted.

All Scripture quotations, unless otherwise indicated, are taken from the Holy Bible, New International Version®, NIV®. Copyright ©1973, 1978, 1984, 2011 by Biblica, Inc.TM Used by permission of Zondervan. All rights reserved worldwide. www.zondervan.com. The "NIV" and "New International Version" are trademarks registered in the United States Patent and Trademark Office by Biblica, Inc.TM

Scripture quotations marked (ESV) are from the ESV® Bible (The Holy Bible, English Standard Version®), © 2001 by Crossway, a publishing ministry of Good News Publishers. Used by permission. All rights reserved. The ESV text may not be quoted in any publication made available to the public by a Creative Commons license. The ESV may not be translated in whole or in part into any other language.

Scripture quotations marked (NLT) are taken from the Holy Bible, New Living Translation, copyright ©1996, 2004, 2015 by Tyndale House Foundation. Used by permission of Tyndale House Publishers, Carol Stream, Illinois 60188. All rights reserved.

Scripture quotations marked (NKJV) are taken from the Holy Bible, New King James Version, Copyright © 1982 by Thomas Nelson, Inc. Used by permission. All rights reserved.

Scripture quotations marked (AMP) are taken from the Amplified® Bible (AMP), Copyright © 2015 by The Lockman Foundation. Used by permission. lockman.org

Scripture quotations marked (NCV) are taken from the Holy Bible, New Century Version, copyright © 2005 by Thomas Nelson, Inc. Used by permission. All rights reserved.

ISBN - 978-1-952840-73-9

UNITED HOUSE Publishing Clarkston, Michigan
info@unitedhousepublishing.com www.unitedhousepublishing.com
Author Photograph: Pam Bonney
Interior Design: Talitha McGuinness; talitha@unitedhousepublishing.com
Printed in the United States of America 2025 - First Edition

SPECIAL SALES:
Most UNITED HOUSE books are available at special quantity discounts when purchased in bulk by corporations, organizations, and special interest groups. For more information, please email orders@unitedhousepublishing.com.

To Chris, Brooks, Ellie, Leighton, Natalie, Lydia, and Lila,
You all are the heart of this book. You've been a constant pulse of joy in my life of motherhood. Thank you for being my greatest inspiration and for joining me on this beautiful, messy, faith-filled journey.

With unwavering love,
Mom

Full Hands, Full Life

Contents

Introduction 5

Establishing Rhythms 11
Week 1: Forming New Habits 13

Week 2: Finding Daily Serenity 19

Week 3: Forming New Habits 23

Week 4: Fueling Through Nutrition 29

Week 5: Breathing for Freedom 35

Week 6: Setting Your Sights 41

Week 7: Prayer with Purpose 47

Week 8: Working Out 53

Week 9: Serving Others 61

Week 10: Defining your Destiny / Personal Transformation 67

Battling Mindsets 75
Week 11: Negativity / Power of Words 77

Week 12: Unexpected / Failure 83

Week 13: Anxiety 87

Week 14: Self-Image 93

Week 15: Personal Sacrifice 99

Week 16: Disappointment / Curveballs of Life 103

Week 17: Strongholds of Addiction 109

Week 18: Fear 115

Week 19: Perfection Not Needed 119

Week 20: Stay Focused 125

Censoring Influencers 131
Week 21: Find Your People 133

Week 22: Advocate with Doctors 139

Week 23: Minimizing Sibling Rivalry 145

Week 24: Fleeing Generational Curses 151

Week 25: Forgiving the Un-forget-able 157
Week 26: Balancing Comparison 163
Week 27: Managing Family Dynamics 167
Week 28: Facing Comments from Others 173
Week 29: Documenting God Winks 179
Week 30: Beholding Nature's Beauty 183

Mothering Practicalities 189
Week 31: Baby Elephant Syndrome 191
Week 32: Fragility of Infants 197
Week 33: Phases of Life 203
Week 34: Fear Removal 207
Week 35: Natural Motherly Instincts / Postpartum 213
Week 36: Schedule Reliability 217
Week 37: Career + Motherhood 223
Week 38: Parenting Hacks 229
Week 39: New Life Care 237
Week 40: Mirror Images 243

Notes 248
Acknowledgements 252

Introduction

Welcome, friend! I'm excited to embark on this journey with you. The Lord has something special in store for you in the pages of this book. Through decades of mentoring teenagers entering motherhood and my own experience of six pregnancies, I know how common pregnancy and motherhood are connected with anxiety and fear. In John 10:10b, Jesus said "He came to give life to the full." And, in 2 Timothy 1:7, He mentioned not giving us a spirit of fear, but one of power, strength, and a sound mind. He did not follow that up with, except for those bearing children! So, my prayer is that through the pages of this book, you discover a full life and a mind void of anxiety.

Motherhood opens your heart to a love you've never known. As we journey into motherhood, whether with your first or your sixth, every new baby is a gift from the Lord! How inspiring that you are taking steps towards getting things in line now to prepare yourself to embrace the future ahead. What an exciting time in life.

If I'm being completely honest, I am humbled you are holding this book. Perhaps all authors feel this way, but the word "fraud" comes to mind when I think of being an author. I didn't major in English, journalism, or creative writing. I haven't fostered a lifelong love of journaling. I don't boast about having a solid foundation in literary techniques and theory. But, I know where thoughts of self-doubt stem from. I felt the calling on my life to write this devotional, and if it helps set up one mom better to celebrate motherhood and lead the next generation to know Jesus, then I know the Lord spoke to me. As I tell my kids, I will do everything in my power to help them maneuver around the same stumbling blocks that tripped me up along the way. The same is true with your journey into motherhood. Had I been stronger in my faith and known what I know now, I would have taken different steps.

Whether you just saw the positive pregnancy test or have been mothering for as long as you can remember, I am confident your timing in starting this devotion is divine and perfect in your journey. The Lord has something special in store for you.

The devotional is divided into four, ten-week sections. In all, we will be spending forty weeks together. The number forty holds significance. Think about it. The Lord designed the gestation of a human, His only creation bearing His image, to last forty weeks. Noah and his family stayed on the ark forty days and nights before the rain stopped. Moses spent forty years leading people through the wilderness. Jesus was tempted by the devil for forty days and nights in the wilderness. While many Biblical scholars focus on the time of waiting, I'm fired up about what was on the other side—new life! For Noah, it was a fresh start to the world. For Moses, the promised land flowed with milk and honey. But perhaps the most exciting new phase of life (and rightfully so!) is the devil fleeing from Jesus. After forty days of fasting in the desert, Jesus was hungry (and all the pregnant ladies said, "Amen!"). The devil knew exactly how to tempt Jesus. He started with the physical need of hunger by saying, "'If you are the Son of God, tell these stones to become bread.' Jesus answered, 'It is written: Man does not live on bread alone, but on every word that comes from the mouth of God.'" (Matthew 4:3-4 NIV) He then entices Jesus with a spiritual battle by asking Him to test God with His safety by throwing Himself down from the highest point of the temple. Jesus answered, "Do not put the Lord your God to the test."(Matthew 4:7) The devil's final attempt at throwing Jesus off His game involved promising Him power over all the kingdoms of the world. Jesus, even in His hungry, nutrient depleted state replied perfectly with, "Away from me, Satan! For it is written: 'Worship the Lord your God, and serve him only.' Immediately the devil left him, and angels came and attended him."(Matthew 4:10-11)

How powerful! After being tempted in all the ways we experience temptations daily—physical needs, mental battles, power struggles—Jesus shows that in His name the devil flees! Jesus gets to start His new purpose of preaching and ministering in the power of the Holy Spirit after the devil flees. Jesus's success in resisting the temptation of the devil ultimately leads us together on a quest to birth our new, full life Jesus promised us in John 10:10.

In the same length of time it takes for a new human to be formed, we have the opportunity to give birth to a new, healthy perspective on our roles as mothers, full of hope and promise. Pregnancy and motherhood are flooded with the unexpected and the unplanned. Those two factors, mixed with raging hormones, create a breeding ground for anxiety and self-doubt. This devotional provides a roadmap to put guardrails in place to keep our minds from being pulled down into the gutter of isolation and despair.

To dive deeper into the weekly devotional topics, I highly recommend coupling this book with the Full Hands, Full Life Activity Companion Guide. The following five interactive, weekly activities, found in the Companion Guide, invite you to explore the devotional topics and scripture in tangible, memorable ways.

1. Journaling Prompts
   Thought provoking questions and space to write your own responses to process through the week's topic.

2. Scripture Art
   A beautiful masterpiece you can create while you turn down the noise of life and perhaps even memorize the scripture for the week.

3. Music Meditation
   A worship song selected that invites you to experience the thoughts and scripture focus for the week. May the gifts of these artists be music to your soul!

4. Prayer Prompts
   Sometimes finding the right words to say is just out of reach. These prayers create a launching point into an ongoing conversation that follows the direction of your heart each week.

5. Future Dreaming
   With prompts for each week, this space creates an area

to jot down memories you never want to forget, whether they are developmental milestones in your children, memories from your own childhood you want to share with them, or dreams you hold for your future together.

While pregnant with my first, I was reading through the New Testament. Being an avid journaler at heart (meaning I love the idea of journaling but never created space in my schedule to actually put pen to paper), I jotted down how many weeks pregnant I was while reading. So, on the first page of Phillippians in my Bible, it says "Week 28." What took me two seconds to jot down has brought back fond memories of that time period in my life for fifteen years already. My hope is that our weekly experiential activities detailed above provide a space for fellow "journalers at heart." I am forever wishing I documented more moments through the years because now I struggle to remember when I felt the first kicks, which child had hiccups at 3pm every day, or how old they were when they first smiled, crawled, or gave me the first drool dripping, open-mouthed kiss (if you don't know—you soon will!). If I had created a space for these bullet-pointed memories, I would cherish them now.

We will spend our forty weeks together combatting, strengthening, and fortifying ourselves with Biblical truths we can hold on to and the factors in our control, so that when the desert seasons come, our storehouse of water is built up to supply our needs. We will be the transformed mothers our littles need. It's going to take some work. It's going to take some time. It's going to take some soul revival. But on the other side of these forty weeks, my prayer is for you to be walking in your transformed life.

What this devotion will not be is a guide for all-natural child birth or early signs of labor. See, I've never experienced either. As a mom of six, I don't have the "all natural, forget the pain right after childbirth" stories that so many women share. I birthed these little humans into the world through six C-sections. More on those in the pages to follow, but just know that these new life revival tips are vetted, tried, tested, and true from a fellow mom who shows up with my crew at Walmart and gets looked at like a walking circus act.

What I pray you will find as you move through this devotional is an undeniable feeling that the God who created the Earth and everything in it loves you and your children an immeasurable amount. The Bible says we are created in God's own image (Genesis 1:26), and He loves you so much that He is now entrusting you with not only bearing His image, but also carrying and growing His image.

Maybe you've never heard this and maybe it will be something hard to believe, but let me be perhaps the first to share this truth with you at the onset of our time together: You are worthy of bringing your children into this world. The Lord said, "You are precious in my eyes, and honored, and I love you" (Isaiah 43:4). You are welcomed into being excited about being a mom in whatever capacity that will take. God specializes in making beauty from ashes (Isaiah 61:3). There is redemption in every story the Lord's hand is in, and since this book has found its way to yours, the Lord is writing His way into your story.

I want to pause and pray for you, and the journey set out before you.

Lord Jesus,

Thank You. Thank You for the beautiful life that now holds this book. Thank You for the beautiful life bearing Your image that these mothers are growing. Lord, hold them both in Your arms. Let this devotion be a gift to her soul. Let the giftings You blessed her with become evident in these pages. Show up in her life in magnificent ways over the next forty weeks—undeniable ways, Lord, that only point to Your goodness, Your mercy, and Your peace. Let this precious woman come out victorious in her new, full life on the other side of these forty weeks. We love You and are believing and standing firm on Your promises, Father God. We pray all of this in Your precious son, Jesus' name.

Amen.

Now let's rewrite the thoughts which run through our minds about pregnancy and motherhood. Onward, friend, fellow image bearer of Christ himself.

Weeks 1-10
Establishing Rhythms

Full Hands, Full Life

Week 1: Forming New Habits

Are you ready?! We're jumping into Week 1 of this new life revival. I'm ready, I'm excited, and I have the perspective of knowing the freedom and peace the Lord has promised for you at the end of this forty week journey.

If you're wondering why forty weeks, I'd love for you to take a moment and read the Introduction. Maybe you are like me. You fit twenty-five hours into every twenty-four hour day. You want to jump into the meat of the topic, get to the good stuff, avoid the fluff, so you skip over the Intro. If so, I extend to you total grace! Please realize this devotional is written by someone with the same mindset. Hand over my heart, I promise you will find no fluff in these pages. I believe the Lord has something for you even in the Intro! So, I'll patiently wait here for you while you turn back and give it a quick read.

Ok, now I'm ready, and you're ready! At some point along this forty week journey, you may birth a new life into this world. Perhaps you will move or your children will start a new school year. Regardless of how far along you are on this motherhood journey, change is inevitable.

Routines will change. Needs will change. My prayer is for this devotional and the accompanying activity companion guide to be something consistent through the change for you to cling to and give you peace. May they become a constant amidst the change, helping you ground yourself in establishing new rhythms which can be continued into motherhood.

Like learning any new skill, transforming your mind is going to take time and practice. Hear me say, "Practice doesn't make perfect. Practice makes progress." Free yourself from the pressure of perfection in this study. You can jump through the week's activities based on what your week holds and the spaces you find available for soul work. The activities are titled as such. Perhaps you take several days to complete an activity. Perhaps an activity really speaks to your heart and you come back to it multiple times during the week. This is your journey, so let the Spirit lead you through the nudging of your heart on when to move forward and when to abide.

Establishing the habit of continual mind transformation is vitally important. Habits, good or bad, are being formed in your life whether you are conscious of them or not. For example: Do you set your alarm twenty minutes early so you can snooze two times? Do you scroll reels before falling asleep at night? Do you put on your seatbelt before leaving the parking spot? The 21/90 rule states that it takes twenty-one days to make a habit and ninety days to make it a permanent lifestyle change. Think about how many twenty-one and ninety day periods we have already had in our life up until this point.

What are some of the habits we have already formed simply from daily living? Commit to your goal for twenty-one days, and it will become a habit. Over time, habits become lifestyle choices.

By jumping into this devotional, you have demonstrated a desire for a new lifestyle choice, a new habit. When I was pregnant with my first, our only son to date, my pregnancy was plagued with low amniotic fluid. Amniotic fluid is the liquid surrounding the baby that serves as a cushion for the baby. More importantly, it serves to facilitate the exchange of nutrients, water, and biochemical products between the mother and growing baby.

Each OB check-up appointment, I measured weeks smaller than I was supposed to. If you are in this space, I totally get the emotional rollercoaster you are going through! Checkup after checkup, I sat on hard benches in the cold hallways outside the ultrasonographer's room waiting for space in her schedule to open up to check on the growth of Brooks. While I loved the extra opportunities to see the precious baby boy I had been feeling wiggle around, I loathed the periods of wild thoughts running through my mind during the waiting. Was I doing something prohibiting his ability to grow? Would this be the week I was rushed in for an emergency delivery?

Brooks was due in late July. The end of my pregnancy was spent during the hottest months of the year. In North Carolina, temperature and humidity increase proportionally—the higher the temperature, the higher the humidity. By late July, the air outside is thick, sometimes feeling like you must swim through it. We joke about there being weeks in the summer when the only explanation for being outside is if water activities are involved. In this kind of environment, pregnant women are increasingly susceptible to dehydration and heat stroke.

During one of my appointments, my doctor mentioned amniotic fluid is 98% water and 2% salt and cells from the baby, so the best way to increase my amniotic fluid was to intake more water. A light bulb went off. I needed to create a new habit of drinking more water. Every time I brushed my teeth, I began drinking a full glass of water. At least twice a day I was getting more water with very little change in my daily routine. Now fifteen years later, this is a lifestyle norm for me. Even when I stay in a hotel, I seek out the plastic covered glasses and put one next to the sink.

Experiencing lifestyle changes works well when paired with existing daily routines. For me, the time and space was already set aside for brushing my teeth. Adding a cup of water during those times wasn't tough to remember. But, I did have to plan ahead and place a reminder in plain sight—a cup next to the sink. The cup stood out from the rest of the bathroom decor. It was loud, bright, and large. Not the typical disposable Dixie cup kids use for rinsing. If I'm honest, the size of the cup needed to be large enough so I wasn't having to fill it up more than once. Life didn't have time for small cups (remember my 25 hours in every 24 hour day?). Now fifteen years later, I have a Tervis cup with affectionate Mom names written all over it that lives on our bathroom counter. I'm not trying to take this habit analogy too far, but think about how much water this lifestyle choice has added to my life. Water is essential in human life as it flushes waste from the body, regulates body temperature, transports nutrients, and is necessary for digestion. Over the past fifteen years, adding twelve ounces of water at each brushing session, I've increased my intake by 131,400 ounces, over 1025 gallons of water, or enough water to fill up nearly six hot tubs, twenty-three bathtubs, or sixty car gas tanks! That's a lot of water!

Spend this week consciously working through your daily routines. Are there new lifestyle changes you would like to make? Things you would like to add into your daily routines? Lifestyle choices you would like to remove from your routine? First, write them down. Writing them down helps you hold yourself accountable.

The next forty weeks creating a lifestyle marked by consistent, healthy mind renewal are laid out before you! Anyone can start the race, some may make it halfway, but few make it to the end. Commit to being one of the few who cross the finish line. What better reward could you get than life renewal?! Jesus invites us into following Him, to not walk in darkness but to have the light of life (John 8:12). Over the next nine weeks, we will dip our toes into some habits that became paramount lifestyle choices I made over the years that deeply impacted my relationship with the Lord, my joy in parenting, and my ability to experience the light of life.

➡️ ***Jump to pages 4-8 in the***
Full Hands, Full Life Activity Companion Guide
for this week's interactive prompts.

Full Hands, Full Life

Week 2: Finding Daily Serenity

When you think of serenity, what images come to mind? Sitting on the seashore, wind gently blowing your hair from your face? Lying in a hammock, gently rocking back and forth? Diving onto a plush king bed overflowing with pillows being engulfed in a white, down comforter? What colors pair in your mind with serenity—gentle pastels, shades of blue, or an ombre flow among several hues?

For me, a specific feeling goes along with serenity. A sense of calm, security, familiarity, and comfort. Picture being wrapped up in an incredibly soft blanket, my toes just the right temperature in comfy socks. A warmly scented candle is burning just within the periphery, and I hold a perfectly warm pecan praline, caramel macchiato. Ok, I got specific. The space around me is quiet, still, and welcoming.

Now, remember six children live in our home. Although I can close my eyes and picture serenity, when I open them, serenity is the last word I would use to describe my surroundings! As I wrote this chapter, I fled to our porch to escape all the chores calling for my attention—dirty dishes filling the sink, laundry scattered about, legos littering the playroom floor. Sometimes inaudible things even rob us of our serenity. If I'm honest, many times the clutter and responsibilities, the never-ending "to-do" list, inhibits my ability to find serenity.

In my early motherhood years, I went to grad school seeking an MBA—Masters of Business Administration. Much to my surprise, a required psychology elective showed up on the course of study. Now this was not just any psychology course but one designed to drive each student towards introspection. We were urged to figure out more about our inherent tendencies, personal drivers for motivation, and crippling inhibitions, all spun in a direction of being able to maximize our strengths and minimize our weaknesses beyond the workplace. This deep, soul searching course is where I first heard the term ambivert.

Growing up, I was familiar with people being described as introverts or extroverts. Typically introverts were coined as shy, quiet souls, and extroverts were the loud, outgoing type. So, when I showed up for the first day and tested as the third personality type, ambivert, I started digging for explanations. As it turns out, an ambivert has a balance of both introversion and extroversion, but can lean towards one trait or the other within the context of the occasion. In large social gatherings, an ambivert joins in with the conversation, cracks a few jokes, speaks up to voice opinions, and generally gets excited about the opportunity to go out with others. However, when it comes to a person's innate ability to recharge their personal battery, extroverts and introverts differ greatly. After a long week, an extrovert is looking forward to going out Friday night, chatting about the week, or forgetting it all together. An introvert is looking forward to hunkering down, reading a book, watching a show, but most importantly, not being burdened with conversation. On that scale, I'm an extreme introvert. Did I mention I live with six children and one extroverted husband?

Figuring out this hard-wired battery recharge (truthfully, it's sometimes a complete software reboot) instantly brought clarity to so many aspects in life. It explained why after finally getting kids down for the night, I longed to go curl up and read in solitude while my husband sought me out to talk through the latest news he was learning about. For me, finding serenity makes life more balanced—for everyone! On a soul level, I needed to find a few minutes of peace and quiet each day. Believe it or not, God calls us all—introverts, extroverts, and even those ambiverts alike—to be still and listen.

*"Be still before the LORD and wait patiently for him;
do not fret when people succeed in their ways,
when they carry out their wicked schemes."
Psalms 37:7*

*"He says, 'Be still, and know that I am God;'"
Psalms 46:10a*

Being still is contrary to modern society. In a world full of quantifying success through productivity and increased efficiency, we pack every minute to the brim, or experience feelings of guilt and uneasiness with open time. Our natural response to filling silence and loneliness is scrolling through reels, reading through posts, or watching videos. But, our creator encouraged us to be still, wait, and find comfort knowing that He is God. Being still can't happen for me with distractions around. We are all human. We all have a little shiny object, distractible mindset inside. What helped me to be still, and what I hope will help you focus, is seeking out a specific spot where stillness can occur. Maybe it is a quiet room (or closet!) in the house; perhaps it's turning a chair towards your favorite wall of pictures, a piece of artwork, a flower patch in your yard, or a view from a window. Perhaps it is the back seat of your car in the driveway!

The actual space itself is far less important than the consistency in which you arrive there. The space is intended as somewhere you can be alone in your thoughts and invite the Lord to show up. I know—that is sometimes a scary place to go. The word "alone" can drive up the exact opposite emotions and feelings from serenity. Colors change to grays and blacks. Warmth becomes bone-chilling cold. Atmospheres turn from cozy, plush fabrics to hard, uncomfortable surfaces. We sometimes go to drastic measures to avoid being alone, but most times we pacify the discomfort by grabbing our phones. Soon the thoughts and experiences of others pass the time, filling the void.

Beautifully, the Lord is always by our side. We are never alone. He calls us to solitude and stillness so we can settle our thoughts to attune our mind to feel his presence.

One of the most serene promises in all the Bible is not only does the Lord show up to listen and guide us through prayer, he also promises "the peace of God, which transcends all understanding, will guard your hearts and your minds in Christ Jesus" (Philippians 4:7).

Don't we all need more of that? More peace and understanding? More guidance and protection? I don't know about you, but if the God of the universe promises those things for me just by me being still and waiting on him, I'll block off the time in my calendar every single day!

➡️ **Jump to pages 10-14 in the Full Hands, Full Life Activity Companion Guide for this week's interactive prompts.**

Week 3: Reading for Growth

Can I let you in on a little secret? By having this book in your hands (hard copy or digitally!), you are a reader. Yep. Grasp and hold on to that label for life, dear friend. Perhaps you've never dreamed of describing yourself as a "reader." For me, my joy of reading disappeared in high school. That void carried on through college as the reading topics required of me drained my time and energy. I remember reading hundreds of pages of various textbooks, case studies, and novels, all with the lens of being able to provide thought-provoking answers to questions already interpreted by professors who held the gavel on the "correct" response. Far be it from me to have a different opinion or view of something. Is it just me, or did professors find joy in picking out the most minute details to hone in on in hopes of weeding out the truly devoted students from those just skimming by?

If your pathway through school was anything like mine, you may have lost your joy of reading as well. Maybe you still find yourself in the read—write paper—take test—repeat cycle of school right now. The idea of reading something on your own gumption shocks you.

So, why the big push on reading? Let me share some thoughts from incredibly successful pioneers in their fields to shed light on how reading impacts lives.

Oprah Winfrey, American host and television producer, often refers to reading as her "path to freedom." She says, "I learned to read at age 3 and soon discovered there was a whole world to conquer that went beyond our farm in Mississippi."[1] She attested that books widened her imagination to see the world beyond the front porch of her grandmother's shotgun house. She suggested children (aren't we all lifelong children!) make a habit of spending about thirty minutes reading each day.

In an interview with Scholastic, 10-time grammy award winner Taylor Swift shared, "I wouldn't be a songwriter if it wasn't for books that I loved as a kid. I think that when you can escape into a book it trains your imagination to think big and to think that more can exist than what you see."[2]

Cori Arnold, an author and billionaire, infamously shared on a viral TikTok, "I became a millionaire at age 41; I could have become a millionaire by age 34 if I had installed these habits sooner."[3] Do you know which habit she listed in the #1 spot? You guessed it—reading books! She quoted Thomas Crowley's research that claims 85% of financially successful people read at least two books per month.

It's true that nearly every successful person attributes their success to a habit of reading.

Sadly, reading seems to be a fleeting pass-time activity much to the demise of thought leaders. According to the American Psychological Association, one of every three teenagers has not read a book for pleasure in a year.[4] The decreasing interest in reading could lead the next generation to face challenges in achieving both health and affluence.

Research proves how reading positively affects human health and financial security across the board. In a Pew Research study, while 75% of Americans polled had read a book in the last year, the remaining 25% of Americans shared some staggering similarities. The research showed that 39% of the people with a lower level of education (high school diploma or less) reported not having read a book in the past year, while only 11% of those with higher education reported the same. The annual household income seemed to be correlated with the amount of reading done by the people in the household as well: households with incomes of $30,000 or lower are a lot more likely to not read than those with earnings exceeding $75,000 (31% vs 15%).[5]

As your journey into motherhood takes shape, the importance of reading books to set your little blessing up as a successful adult gains focus. Children tend to mimic the habits they see in the home. So, we must be modeling a love for reading! And, it's never too late to develop the love of reading. In Ephesians 4, Paul writes that "You were taught, with regard to your former way of life, to put off your old self, which is being corrupted by its deceitful desires; to be made new in the attitude of your minds; and to put on the new self, created to be like God in true righteousness and holiness."

Perhaps you've never seen yourself as a reader. You would rather spend time relaxing through scrolling or watching TV. Maybe you have other pastimes, or maybe you just don't have time for anything extra. Might I gently suggest taking something out of your schedule? Modeling a love of reading may open up your life to a world of endless possibilities for you and your children.The desires of the flesh will always be calling out to us, but to renew our minds, we have to put on our new self, which means being ok with letting go of patterns of the past.

We've read so many quotes from successful people about how reading played a significant role in their pathway to success. I've found this to be incredibly true in my life as well. In my roles as mom, wife, co-worker and friend, when I'm intentionally reading books and working through spiritual devotionals which strengthen weak areas, that's when I am most prepared to be a light in the life of others. Here are a few books that cross a span of genres and topics which transformed my life. I hope they help catapult you into a love of reading. If purchasing books isn't in your budget these days, check out the local library to see if they have copies of these available!

1. *On Becoming Babywise: Giving Your Infant the GIFT of Nighttime Sleep* by Robert Bucknam M.D. & Gary Ezzo
   My husband and I used this routine with all our babies, and its success in showing us how to get sleep is perhaps a contributing factor to us having six kids! Ha! Naturally syncing up your baby's feeding time, wake time, and nighttime sleep cycles helps the entire family sleep through the night.

2. *Redeeming Love* by Francine Rivers
   Francine Rivers has a God-given ability to set Biblical history in a different time period to give the reader a new perspective into the character of God. Warning: several scenes describe Gomer's life as a prostitute with descriptive imagery. The parallel between Gomer and Hosea's love story and the unconditional, redemptive, all-consuming love of our heavenly Father for us is undeniable.

3. *Think and Grow Rich* by Napoleon Hill
   One of the first books I read on a journey to think outside of the box I put my life in. It kept me evaluating thoughts throughout the day. Originally published in 1937, it explains how a positive mindset and persistence helps achieve success.

4. *The 7 Habits of Highly Effective People* by Stephen Covey
   I love a manageable list. This step-by-step guide helped me value the importance of goal setting and then break down the steps to walk them into being. Originally published in 1989, this book still offers an effective framework for establishing both personal and professional habits.

Before we leave this important topic, I want to share a few short statistics to show a direct correlation between low literacy rates and incarceration.

- 85% of all juveniles who interface with the juvenile court system are functionally low-literate.[6]
- Juvenile incarceration reduces the probability of high school completion and increases the probability of incarceration[7] later in life.
- High school dropouts are 63% more likely to be incarcerated[8] than their peers with four-year college degrees.
- According to the National Adult Literacy Survey, 70% of all incarcerated adults cannot read at a fourth-grade level,[9] "meaning they lack the reading skills to navigate many everyday tasks or hold down anything but lower (paying) jobs."

As mothers, we are strategically positioned to create opportunities for our children to fall in love with reading: taking trips to the library, having accessible books in the home, reading stories aloud, and encouraging reading time over screen time. By doing so, we can take significant steps towards setting our children up to avoid the perils associated with low literacy rates.

Let me share some good news of victory with you! By holding this book, you are already jumping in to establish this rhythm in your new life of peace and confidence. Well done! So, fellow mother and warrior princess in Christ, let's take a daily stand to put off our former way of life. Commit to diving into a book for ten minutes or ten pages a day to help renew our minds.

➡ Jump to pages 16-20 in the Full Hands, Full Life Activity Companion Guide for this week's interactive prompts.

Week 4: Fueling through Nutrition

We've been together a few weeks now, so I can throw out a gross understatement without you discrediting me as a human being, right? Ok, great. Thanks.

Our bodies are amazing creations.

I know, I know. That's not a new revelation to you. But honestly, pause for a moment and think about it. Our eyes can distinguish about ten million different colors. Our taste buds are replaced every ten days. Our noses have the capability of remembering 50,000 different scents. Our bodies shed about 600,000 particles of skin every hour—ok that's gross, but still true and amazing! There are 100,000 miles of blood vessels in an adult human body. That's enough to stretch around the Earth four times! Although that is shocking, even more so is that uncoiled DNA in all the cells of your body stretch ten billion miles—enough to travel to the sun and back fifty times! Amazing, right?!

Well, those stats only scratch the surface of the intricate details the Creator of the universe put into place when He created us. We are the only creations on this planet He made "in his image" (Genesis 1:27). He saved the likeness of Himself for us! God gifted us with the capacity to think, learn, communicate, and control our environment, which separates us from all other creation on planet Earth. All that being said, He also gave us a huge responsibility.

In Ephesians 5:29-30 (ESV), the apostle Paul says, "For no one ever hated his own flesh, but nourishes and cherishes it, just as Christ does the church, because we are members of his body" (emphasis added).

What does nourishing and cherishing mean? Nourishing refers to substances necessary for growth, health, and maintaining good condition. Cherishing means protecting and caring for (someone) lovingly. What this shows me is Christ, God's Son who came to Earth to show us the heart of our Creator, cares about our well-being from the inside out. He wants us to be strong physically, mentally, and emotionally because He values us as essential components of His body.

Would you say you are nourishing and cherishing your body? Are you fueling your body with the right balance of nutrition and intake of water to run at peak performance? These are especially vital questions if you are currently pregnant. Your diet and environmental surroundings flow directly to your growing baby through the bloodstream during the most vulnerable months of growth, but they are also important after birth if you are nursing or taking care of littles. Nutrition either gives us a leg up on our day's responsibilities or hinders it.

My journey through nutrition has been anything but easy. For years at a time, allergic reactions and dietary restrictions for either my babies or husband required meals that were gluten-free, dairy-free, corn-free, low-sodium, apple-free, banana-free, void of any cayenne pepper, or any combination of the aforementioned ingredients. It was exhausting, but I felt called and equipped to help create meals which were nutritious and tasty to help their bodies perform their best.

However, through nearly two decades of either being pregnant or nursing babies, I've found some simple questions to ask myself when I start feeling depleted of energy and running on empty.

* Are you getting enough protein in your diet?

The very origin of the word—from the Greek word protos, meaning "first"—reflects protein's top-shelf status in human nutrition. Women need 2-3 palm-sized portions of protein a day. Experts suggest that pregnant women need 3-4 servings or 75-100 grams. Personally, I find that my body works best when I start my day with a healthy serving of protein in the morning—eggs, sausage, or a protein shake. If I have not had protein at the beginning of the day, I typically get a headache before lunchtime.

* Are you taking your vitamins?

When the kitchen is a wreck at mealtime and kids are in and out, I sometimes forget to take my own vitamins while I remember to remind the six of them, and about lunchtime I can feel my clarity of mind fading. Check with your doctor for a multivitamin recommendation. Some insurance companies and governmental food supplement programs even cover costs for vitamins.

* Are you drinking enough water?

Headaches are an all too common symptom of dehydration for me and a few of my kids. In fact, I can start seeing blind spots in my vision, which I know is a migraine trigger from dehydration. Keeping a bottle of water with me at all times helps combat those headaches before they start. It's recommended that women drink 11.5 cups or 2.7 liters of water per day.

* Are you eating enough fresh fruits and vegetables?

My dad always said that fruit was the dessert the Lord intended for us to eat. I love that, and the statement has so much truth in it. Some fruits are as sweet as desserts yet don't pack the same calories or cause the big sugar rush that most desserts will. Instilling a love for fruit in place of desserts has helped create healthy rhythms for my kids. I much prefer them having an apple or banana after a late dinner than cookies or ice cream. Having natural sugar instead of artificial breaking down in bellies is much easier as you wind down. The recommendation on fruits per day is five palm-sized portions per person. Since our hands grow as we mature into adulthood, you can use the size of your child's hand to determine how much 5 servings of fruit would be for them as well.

Another regular question around the dinner table at our house is, "what green is on your plate?" Leafy greens and green vegetables pack so many vital nutrients that they are non-negotiables in our home. I tell our kids they will thank me someday; it just might not be today. After going through these questions, I can typically gauge where my nutrition is lacking.

One final, big question moms need to evaluate when pregnant or raising children is: Are you staying in a smoke-free environment?

Even second-hand and third-hand smoke are detrimental to your health. Exposure to smoke during pregnancy increases the likelihood of low birth weight and birth defects. Exposure to smoke from birth to five years of age increases likelihood of respiratory infections, ear infections, and asthma attacks. In babies, secondhand smoke can cause sudden infant death syndrome (SIDS). Setting up expectations for maintaining a smoke-free environment for you and your children, although a larger sacrifice for some, could make a lifelong difference in the life of your child. Many times, presenting the statistics to family members provides clarity on the unintended consequences of certain actions. If you are considering approaching family members with this topic, pray for the Lord to open their ears to hear the truth on what you are

Establishing Rhythms

sharing, the invitation to help be a beacon of change for children, and the Holy Spirit to rest on you as you share the invitation to partner in creating a smoke-free environment with grace.

All these questions can seem daunting at first, but choose one of those areas you want to focus on this week. After the week is concluded, your body will be so thankful! It will fuel you to choose another and make it a priority. The number one way to change the way our body feels is to change how we are fueling it.

➡ Jump to pages 22-26 in the Full Hands, Full Life Activity Companion Guide for this week's interactive prompts.

Week 5: Breathing for Freedom

Let's start this week out with a little riddle, shall we? I'm as light as a feather, yet no one can hold me for long. What am I? Breath. You got it! Ok, perhaps this week's title "Breathing for Freedom" gave you a major clue, but just go ahead and put that in the win column for today.

Oxygen is vital to the health and wellbeing of our bodies. Perhaps you are like me and take this involuntary reflex of the body for granted. Not worrying about remembering to breathe is, in fact, a luxury. You see, everyday functions of the body like digesting your food, moving your muscles, or even just thinking all require oxygen. Not to get all scientific on you, but when these processes happen, carbon dioxide is produced as a waste product. The job of your lungs is to provide your body with oxygen and to get rid of the waste gas, carbon dioxide. Your brain alone uses twenty percent of the total oxygen and blood in your body. In a lifetime, this oxygen helps your brain's long-term memory hold as many as 1 quadrillion (1 million billion) separate bits of information!

Take professional athletes for instance. Hyperbaric

oxygen tanks are commonly used by professional athletes as part of their post-performance recovery. Pulmonologists found supersaturation of a healing body with oxygen showed health benefits, including increased energy and stamina, optimized cellular health, better wound healing, improved cognitive function, and pain relief. With these proven benefits, it should come as no surprise that athletes like Michael Phelps, the most decorated Olympian to date; LeBron James, one of the most successful basketball players to step foot on the court; and Simone Biles, widely considered one of the greatest gymnasts of all time, embrace hyperbaric oxygen therapy as part of their training regimen. Serena Williams, one of the greatest tennis players worldwide, even has a hyperbaric oxygen chamber in her home!

Additionally, hyperbaric oxygen therapy has worked its way into the healthcare sector. One particular research study concluded that patients following a dedicated hyperbaric oxygen therapy protocol experienced more effective pain management and healing from the chronic illness, fibromyalgia, than those following pharmacology (drug) treatments. This difference in approach led to healing damaged brain tissue, curing the chronic illness, instead of just treating the symptoms.[10]

Now I'm going to step out on a limb and assume the majority of us traveling through this new life journey together do not have hyperbaric oxygen tanks at our disposal. Thankfully, the Lord created the atmosphere all around us saturated in the one thing we need for self healing: oxygen. Taking a few slow, deep breaths in succession dramatically increases the amount of oxygen absorbed by the body. With this resource being available to us right where we sit now, establishing a rhythm of breathing seemed to naturally fit in this section of our journey.

The invitation to breathe runs deep in our family. My husband has been telling our kids to breathe through situations of discomfort for years! It honestly used to irk me that his constant response was, "Just breathe." But, the data points to the success in this advice. Now we hear our children encouraging each other to do the same. Stub your toe? Breathe. Nervous to go on stage? Take a few deep breaths. Feel nauseous? Slowly just focus on your breath. Need to pee for the third time on a long road trip when we are miles away from the next exit? Just breathe more space into that bladder! (Just a hypothetical one here, of course...ha!).

However frustrating these simple responses may seem in the moment, this physical response to pain and feelings of discomfort is very warranted. Everything you read about anxiety and depression talks about the power of breathing techniques. Louie Giglio, pastor and leader of Passion City Church, is a self-named anxiety overcomer. In his collection of talks entitled "Putting an 'X' Through Anxiety," he covered this topic of breathing that brought him new life. During stressful situations, his wife taps him on the shoulder and tells him to breathe, because our natural instinct is to hold our breath—the exact opposite of what will help the most. In his first talk in the series, Giglio quotes the American Institute of Stress, saying, "Deep breathing increases the supply of oxygen to your brain and stimulates the parasympathetic nervous system, which promotes a state of calmness. Breathing techniques help you feel connected to your body. It brings awareness away from the worries in your head and quiets your mind." Giglio further explains, "God wants us to get back in touch with our breathing."[11]

God didn't hardwire our bodies to require running marathons every month, eating unseasoned kale for a week, or even sleeping for twenty-four hours straight to find a reset button. He calls us to breathe—something we can do whenever, wherever, for any length of time. Praise Jesus! I don't know about you, but if it were any of the previous three, I'd be out!

So, what does breathing for freedom look like? How can we invite our kids into breathing for healing? It requires quieting your mind to focus on your breath, not only the exhales, but more importantly the inhales. This takes a bit of practice, but our body naturally exhales toxic carbon dioxide and inhales life-giving oxygen. So, what we focus on is breathing out the toxic stressors in life and breathing in the promises of our loving, heavenly Father—all while actually breathing.

The Lord showed time and time again that He speaks to what is dead and breathes life into it. In Genesis 2:7, the Lord "formed man (Adam) from dust and then breathed into his nostrils the breath of life, and the man became a living being." In Ezekiel 37:1-14, the Lord brought a whole valley of dry bones to life through breath. After Jesus' resurrection, He appeared to the disciples and breathed the Holy Spirit into them, giving them new life. This need for breath is fundamental to our health, and not only of our physical bodies but also our mental and spiritual health. The average adult exhales 20,000 times a day. Strong exhales are involuntary to us and often signify thoughts like, "I'm exhausted," "I've had enough," "Not again," "Wow, that was close," or "Thank goodness he or she finally left."

Let's run through a breathing exercise together that you can also use with your family. Quiet the room around you, and listen to the miraculous breath of God in your lungs. Take a moment to acknowledge the things that are worrying you. Things that are weighing heavily on your heart. "I can't take another day of this..." "I don't know what delivery will be like..." "I can't control how my family is feeling about..." "I'm not strong enough to be a mom..." Get in touch with these 20,000 exhales. What are we breathing out? What weights and pressures are we letting go? It's important to put those thoughts into words, but more importantly, we need to get in touch with what the Lord is inviting us to inhale back in, which I can assure you is not more stress, worthlessness, or feelings of instability.

Establishing Rhythms

As you read these prompts, I want you to modify them as needed to fit the thoughts running through your head. Exhale "I can't..." Inhale "...but You can." "I don't... but You do." "I'm not... but You are." When we learn the rhythm of pinpointing and exhaling what we are afraid of, what is holding us back, and breathing in the promises of the One who is greater than any of our weaknesses and capable of more than we could ever imagine, we find freedom. It doesn't rest all on our shoulders. The Lord never created us for the weight of that burden (Matthew 11:28-30).

This week, I want us to meditate over the following prayer Paul prayed over the followers of Jesus in Ephesus.

"I pray that from His (God's) glorious, unlimited resources he will empower you with inner strength through his Spirit. Then Christ will make his home in your hearts as you trust in him. Your roots will grow down into God's love and keep you strong. And may you have the power to understand, as all God's people should, how wide, how long, how high, and how deep his love is. May you experience the love of Christ, though it is too great to understand fully. Then you will be made complete with all the fullness of life and power that comes from God."
Ephesians 3:16-19 (NLT)

Focus on the unlimited resource we have to oxygen all around us and how the Lord is inviting you to breathe in His strength in your weakness and His provision in your deficits. The more we breathe in these truths, these life-giving oxygen moments, the deeper our love for our Father and inner peace will grow.

➡️ **Jump to pages 28-32 in the Full Hands, Full Life Activity Companion Guide for this week's interactive prompts.**

Week 6: Setting Your Sights

Have you ever watched a scary movie, then immediately tried falling asleep? You jump up wide-eyed with every creak of the house. Everything in your room strangely becomes an optional defense weapon you could use along your escape route. You dread having to walk around, but when you do, you turn on every light between your bed and the bathroom.

If you haven't experienced this, you are not missing a thing! I've personally avoided horror films (even their commercials!) since early high school and learned to hit the mute button to drown out the suspenseful music well before that. I learned the negative side effects of sleepless nights early in life. Sleep was far too important. Perhaps the Lord shielded me from those sleepless nights so I could withstand a decade and a half of infants in our home!

What I've noticed over the years is the more positive, uplifting quotes I see, movies I watch, scripture I read and success stories I hear, the more positive my outlook on life remains even amidst tragedy. Seeing the glass half full in all situations is a gift which can be developed. It can be learned, honed in on, and grown. Being able to see the rose from the thorns, and help others find their roses, brings my heart a level of gratitude I didn't experience decades ago. I always keep in mind what my mother-in-law said to me years ago, "People will remember how you make them feel when they are around you, not necessarily what you say." Thankfully, I started taking strides towards this perspective in life before a pivotal moment in my professional career in 2016.

While starting my Masters Degree in Business Administration in 2007, I ran into a former waitress friend, Melissa, during orientation. A few short weeks into the semester, she offered me a position on her team at the healthcare technology start-up business where she worked. My appointed title was Social Butterfly. That title reflects the culture of the company more than my role within it—we were a family. From a stocked kitchen in the penthouse business suite to a break room with bean bag chairs and gaming tables, the company understood the delicate balance of setting high expectations and rewarding high performers.

After seven years with the company, I had climbed the corporate ladder as my job description grew to cover client training, account management, accounts receivables, client liaison between IT development and product placement, and sales and marketing. Even with the professional success, I missed my kids on a daily basis and dreamed of having more time with them.

In the fall of 2015, I went on maternity leave to bring our fourth child, Natalie, into the world. During those twelve weeks, a large company based out of one of the largest cities in the US purchased our company. Upon returning to work, my new role fell into the marketing silo. Marketing constituted the smallest percentage of time previously spent while representing the highest percent of stress and feelings of inadequacy in my day-to-day responsibilities. I constantly felt insecurities creep in, but chose to find joy in learning new skills and conquering challenges week after week. But, I also experienced loneliness. My work silo consisted of a team local to the metropolitan area and virtual me.

In May of 2016, the new company called all remote employees based in our region (which was everyone from the buyout!) together for an all-day Human Resources meeting. Excited for a day with co-workers who felt like family, I trudged in with everything I needed—my computer bag, my purse, my breast pump, my cooler with freezer packs for my milk, and of course, snacks. Every nursing momma needs snacks!

My individual meeting happened first. The Chief Human Resources Officer (CHRO), who had flown down for the meeting, called me to a side room to go over "paperwork." In this room, under hushed tones, he explained that the marketing division was being relocated exclusively to their main hub and they had prepared a severance package for me. I was being let go! The only employee affected by this move was me. But, with how tight knit our previous work family had been, they wanted to manage the fall out in-person. I remember going over the generous severance package and smiling at him in a fog, worried about what my teammates were feeling in the room next door. Then the previous CEO of our local healthcare technology company came in to check on me. Through tear-filled eyes, he uttered, "I'm so sorry." It shook me to the core. The only hesitation he had in selling was having to lose his people. At that moment, I looked him square in the eyes and said, "Don't worry about me! I'm going to be fine. The Lord has a plan for my life. He knows what's next. This wasn't your fault." I honestly shocked myself! My normal flight or flight response is fight, puff-up, and get loud. In that moment, the peace and security of Christ washed over me like I had never experienced before.

Our team pulled together briefly as I went back in the room. There were tears—angry tears from some—and widespread disbelief. Knowing how close we all were, the CHRO gave everyone the rest of the day off and encouraged us to grab lunch downtown together one last time. So, as quickly as humanly possible I packaged up all five bags of belongings, threw them over my shoulders, and we crammed ourselves into the elevator heading downstairs.

The moment I stepped foot from that building, my cell phone rang. In desperation of wanting to escape the situation and collect myself, I asked a coworker to rummage around in the purse flung over my shoulder to find my cell phone. I didn't know who was calling, but I knew whoever it was I needed to talk to them, step away for a moment, and emotionally disconnect from my current life crisis.

On the other end of the line, a woman from the local Christian private school that my son attended started with, "everything is fine with Brooks, but... this may be a long shot... we have a few openings here at the school in the fall and think they may be a perfect fit for you. Do you have any time in your schedule to come in and hear more about them?"

A huge smile of relief spread across my face. Praise Jesus! He did have a plan! He knew what was coming down the pipeline for me and my family. The severance package paid my entire summer vacation, and I started the job at the school without missing a paycheck. The new role cut my pay in half but significantly increased my quality in motherhood. Most importantly, it gave me the opportunity to put my faith in the Lord financially and step into His calling on my life. Nearly a decade later, things have continued evolving vocationally. I no longer work at a school but get the privilege of homeschooling our children. I no longer work in corporate America, but I help run our family-owned recording company with my husband. I no longer run a team of employees, but I get to encourage a team of mentors as we encourage young moms to be the mothers God created them to be. Sometimes the Lord has to close doors for us to see the doors that are wide open, inviting us to walk through them.

However, if we aren't careful, we can cloud our minds with things of this world and miss these heavenly opportunities. Had I missed opportunities to create a friendship with Melissa during shifts at Outback, she may have dismissed me in grad school. Had I not worked hard for a company I may have not made it through the buy-out while on maternity leave. Had I not spoken life and encouraged administration and teachers at the private school, my name may not have come up in conversations for the new position. Interactions with others matter. And, how we set up our minds before being around others matters even more.

So, this week, I want you to take stock of what your sights are on. What are you witnessing, watching, and reading day in and day out? Are they things that edify the life you want to live, or are they things that are holding you captive in your current state?

Colossians 3:1-2 encourages us to "...set our hearts on things above, where Christ is, seated at the right hand of God. Set your minds on things above, not on earthly things." If I watch something where the guy is treating the girl in a deplorable way, it affects the way I look at my husband—as if he had something to do with the story line!
As women, the Lord gifted us to be in tune with our emotions. He crafted us with the emotional capacity to keep a pulse on the connectedness between people because of our God-given ability to nurture little ones. With that comes a great responsibility.

Many times the Lord's plan is crystal clear in hindsight but undetectable in the moment. By keeping our sights on things glorifying Him in this world, we will gain more clarity in the path He has in store for us. Remember we are working towards that John 10:10 promise of living a life to the full. He has one in store for us, so do all you can to not let little daily choices stop you short of yours.

➡ Jump to pages 34-38 in the
Full Hands, Full Life Activity Companion Guide
for this week's interactive prompts.

Week 7: Prayer with Purpose

Have you seen the phrase, "I was today years old when I learned..." on social media recently? Perhaps this phrase has fizzled out, but its original use was to humorously convey the discovery of a new idea or fact. I remember having this type of "Aha!" moment in my late 30's about something I thought I should have known for decades.

While reading Sheila Walsh's book, Praying Women, she expertly detailed how to use scripture to outline prayers. She even went as far as to say when you don't know what to pray, open up Proverbs and start reading them as prayers until something stirs in your heart.

When I read this outline for prayer, it was as if a cue card for screeching tires flashed in my mind. Wait, what? Pray using scripture?! After years and years of teachers warning me of the legal and social ramifications from plagiarizing, this felt like the ultimate crime of stealing. Why would the God of the universe, who wrote the Bible and inspired every single word within the pages, want me to read them back to Him? Doesn't He want me to come up with something creative, something new to convey to Him?

Quite the contrary.

Jesus, who is God in the flesh, His very own Son, humbled Himself and entered life as a precious baby (Phillippians 2:6-8). As we read the New Testament Gospels, the first four books in the second portion of the Bible (Matthew, Mark, Luke, and John), we get a firsthand account of how Jesus interacted with people on the Earth. Most times, we hear about how Jesus interacted with those in society who were the outcasts, seen as less-than citizens, those not worthy to be included with the "in" crowd. And, we also got to see how He entered into a relationship with His heavenly father, our God. As He prayed and spoke with God, Jesus often quoted Old Testament scripture. He quoted Himself!

Perhaps this is a screeching tire moment for you as well, so let me back up a bit. See, Jesus was The Word. The Gospel of John starts off very differently than any of the other Gospels. Most Gospels start with lineage or setting the scene of Mary (nine months pregnant) and Joseph traveling to Bethlehem, riding on a donkey (let me mention again that Mary was nine months pregnant...bless her soul!) to find no room in the inn. So, little baby Jesus was born in a stable, wrapped in swaddling cloths, and laid in a hard, cold, stone, dirty, feeding trough for livestock. Is that story familiar to you?

Well, John starts into his Gospel very differently: "In the beginning was the Word, and the Word was with God, and the Word was God. He was with God in the beginning." Y'all, those capitalizations are not a typo! The word, Word, is capitalized because it is another name for Jesus. Throughout the New Testament, anytime Jesus is mentioned, His name or reference as "He, His, Him, His, etc." is capitalized. In this instance, Jesus is explained as being present in the beginning of all creation. John continues by declaring everything was made through Jesus. Without Jesus in the beginning, the Words of God's thoughts (i.e. "Let there be light") would never have been spoken, and the Earth as we know it today would not have been formed. So all the words of the Word—the Bible—are Jesus and God inspired! So, when Jesus quotes scripture, He is quoting Himself. At the same time, He is exemplifying how it is pleasing to His (and our) Heavenly Father for us to use scripture as a blueprint when we pray as well.

The Bible was created as God's love letter to each of us. The words on the pages are life-breathing, soul-freeing, and awe-inspiring messages we can read again and again and again. The same scripture I read at one point of my life will land completely differently with me at another point in my life.

One of my favorite questions to ask the teenagers I do ministry with is, "What's your favorite type of movie? Action, Drama, Chick Flick, Horror, Comedy?" My answer to whatever kind of movie they say is, "Oh awesome—then you'll love the Bible!" Without fail, they give me the confused puppy dog look, "What?" But, it's true! The Bible has story lines throughout that check all of the favorite genres of movies and then some!

This realization that praying scripture back to Jesus is a compliment and shows my understanding of His love letter written to me blew my mind. My prayers have never been the same since. It's like the "putting peanut butter on the insides of both pieces of bread before the jelly keeps the bread from ever getting soggy" kind of realization which prevents you from going back to making lunchbox PB&Js any other way. In other words, it was life changing.

As Jodie Berndt, author of Praying the Scriptures for Your Children, beautifully explains, "Talking to God—the One who knows us better and loves us more than anyone else in the world—should be a natural thing".[12] She suggests thinking of scriptures as promises you can use in a conversation with God as a launching point.

I know prayers have been included each week thus far, but I'd love to provide some prayers you can start lifting up this week that are pulled directly from scripture. Checking out different versions of the Bible can be helpful when you are starting to use scripture as a blueprint for prayers. Using something like the Bible App or BibleHub.com helps you easily toggle between different versions of the Bible (some that I like using are the New International Version, The Message, English Standard Version 2016, New Living Translation, and The Amplified) providing more insights and clarity on verses. For many of these prayers below I have used The Amplified version of the Bible, which writes verses in a way that mimics everyday conversations.

Knowing What to Pray

Dear God,
Thank You for giving me Your Holy Spirit to help me when I don't know how to pray (Romans 8:26). Help me be alert and always keep praying for people. (Ephesians 6:18) Today I want to pray for _____ . Amen.

For Direction in Life

Lord,
Show me the path You have for my life; Help me find joy in Your presence (Psalm 16:11).

For Your Children's Protection & Safety

Heavenly Father,
Keep _____ from all harm. Watch over their coming and going, both now and forevermore (Psalm 121:7-8).

Lord,
I pray that in every way _____ may succeed and prosper and be in good health [physically] (3 John 1:2).

Heavenly Father,
Let _____ lie down and sleep in peace (Psalm 4:8). (All new mommas said, "Amen!")

For Your Child's Future Spouse

It's never too early to start praying for their spouses! On average, husbands and wives were only 2.2 years apart in age in 2022, regardless of which spouse is older.[13] So, it is highly likely your child's spouse will be conceived before they are a year and a half and born before they are twenty-eight months old! This is true for my husband and I. Although we don't follow the social norms with me being older than him, we are only fourteen months apart. Thankfully his momma started praying for me from day one!

Heavenly Father,
Help _____ and his/her future spouse be willing to wait for Your perfect timing in finding a marriage partner, even as Jacob waited seven years to marry Rachel. Let the waiting period seem to go by quickly, as You kindly did for Jacob (Genesis 29:20).

God,
Let the peace of Christ [the inner calm of one who walks daily with Him] be the controlling factor in _____'s heart and my future daughter-in-law/son-in-law's heart [deciding and settling questions that arise] with Your peace along the way. And lead them to be thankful to You for finding each other when the day arrives (Colossians 3:15).

For Patience and Self-Control

Lord,
I believe You have chosen me and called me by name, that I am holy [set apart, sanctified for your purpose] and well-beloved [by You], so Lord I ask for You to help me put on a heart of compassion, kindness, humility, gentleness, and patience to endure whatever is to come with a good temper. On my own, I would not be able to. Thank You (Colossians 3:12).

I hope you can use these prayers as a launching point to start these honest conversations with the Lord. To keep our minds focused on the frequency in which we are encouraged to pray, our scripture for this week comes from a blessing Paul wrote to the people of Philippi. It has become one of the most quoted scriptures of all time. And, at the center of this verse is the call to take our worries, cares, and desires to the feet of Jesus through prayer. Nothing is too small (or too big!) to talk about with God. Unlike us, He's never overwhelmed, too busy, or weary. He never falls asleep mid-conversation or rolls His eyes when we call out His name. In fact, He is never so distracted that we have to call his name out twice (or three times!). He is waiting, even right now, for us to start a conversation with him.

> "Do not be anxious or worried about anything, but in everything [every circumstance and situation], by prayer and petition with thanksgiving, continue to make your [specific] requests known to God. And the peace of God [the peace which reassures the heart] which transcends all understanding, [the peace which] stands guard over your hearts and your minds in Christ Jesus [is yours]."
> Philippians 4:6-7 (Amplified)

➡ Jump to pages 40-44 in the Full Hands, Full Life Activity Companion Guide for this week's interactive prompts.

Week 8: Working Out

Let's be honest. Did this week's title make you want to skip immediately to week nine, or even worse, quit our forty week journey altogether? I hope not! The focus of this week is not to condemn those of us who have never stepped foot in the gym (outside of the required high school physical education course). The goal is to help us all find a healthy rhythm of activity in our daily lives after unpacking the "why"?

If you had to choose from the following list, how would you classify yourself (and be honest—I didn't ask how you "should" classify yourself!)

- The "Avid Worker-Outer" ~ *The day is a failure if I don't get in my reps.*
- The "Can Dress the Part-er" ~ *I've got the fits, but they're to lounge in, not lunge in.*
- The "New Years Resolution Lifer" ~ *This time I'll stick to this new workout routine.*
- The "Team Sporter" ~ *Why work out when you can play to sweat?*
- The "Maybe Next Year-er" ~ *This season is too challenging, but I'll have time soon!*

Perhaps there's a different way you would classify your outlook on working out, but the majority of us would fall into one of those five categories. The beauty of working out is that it can look completely different in each of our lives. I personally know nothing about being a "Team Sporter," aside from a short stint of playing co-ed softball with my husband one season—sorry, Chris! I was the catcher, which sounds really important. After all, there is only one person on a team who gets the title of catcher. There are plenty of outfielders! But, I quickly learned that in co-ed, couples softball, the catcher is where they hide the weakest, most unreliable player on the team. The game probably would have gone faster with me standing back at the fence behind home plate and grabbing the ball each time, had I been able to throw it hard enough to get it back to the pitcher from way back there! But, instead, I did what I like to refer to as the "lady catcher dance." I did a little squat down, would reach towards the ball flying at my face, close my eyes as I flinched, all while trying not to get hit by the fiberglass bat or ironically hard softball. Then, I would open my eyes to find the ball rolling towards the fence, missing my glove over 95% of the time. Pop up. Jog back to get the ball, and jog back to the plate (well, jogging turned to walking by inning four) so I could attempt to throw it back to the pitcher every single pitch. How exhausting!

One Sunday evening, I shocked the team. The pitcher threw a beautiful drop ball pitch (okay—I have no idea what kind of pitch it actually was, but doesn't it sound so official?). It was zeroing in on the strike zone. The left-handed batter swung what looked to be an ideal swing, but at the last second the ball dropped nicking the bottom of the batter's bat, bouncing it straight down to home plate. Not sure if you know this, but softballs bounce—like, a LOT. That ball hit the plate so hard it came straight up to my face. I started the normal flinch, close-my-eyes-lady-catcher-dance-routine, but simultaneously reflexes took over, and my glove shot above my head. That hard softball landed square in my glove... and I didn't drop it! In the moment, a flood of adrenaline overtook all my sensibilities, and I pumped my chest out, threw my arms out wide and yelled, "Yeah!" as if to say, "Look, all you haters. Today, you just witnessed glory. You are welcome that I chose to grace you all with my presence." That was the only day they witnessed that glory because the next game a similar situation happened. Drop ball bounced off home and came up square under my chin. Did I mention yet that I had NO catcher's equipment? No padding. No helmet. The shock of taking that cannon of a shot under my jaw made my ears ring and my confidence plummet. That pain, along with the facial bruising, was the start of the quick end to our co-ed softball days.

So, no—I wouldn't classify myself as a "Team Sporter." I'm more of an "Avid Worker-Outer" to a fault. More on the mental battles I've had as a female coming up in quarter two of our journey, but for now, let's just say negative self-talk is known to play in my mind if my balance of working out and stress are not kept in check. As the level of stress in my life increases (remember I am a mother of six children, work multiple jobs, and homeschool), I can spiral pretty quickly into being a hot-tempered, impatient, and impulsive mess. Working out helps combat that tendency.

The Center for Disease Control and Prevention states, "Regular physical activity is one of the most important things you can do for your health. Being physically active can improve your brain health, help manage weight, reduce the risk of disease, strengthen bones and muscles, and improve your ability to do everyday activities."[14] In fact, other benefits of physical activity include:

* Reduced risk of depression and anxiety
* Reduced risk of type 2 diabetes and metabolic syndrome
* Better sleep
* Lowered risk for developing several types of cancer
* Strengthened bones, joints, and muscles
* Increased chances of living longer

For the sake of our time together, I'll stop the list there, but there is no shortage of studies or proven research on the benefits of physical activity. So, why can it be so tough to work this into our daily rhythms? I believe one factor is because the box we fit working out in is too small. Working out does not have to mean getting dressed, getting in a car or bus or taking the metro to get all sweaty around the grunters and machine hoggers in the gym. If that is your scene, awesome. Keep at it! But, for others, that's not a good fit. Thankfully that's not the only option.

Working physical activity into your daily routine can be electing to take the stairs instead of the elevator in your apartment building or at work. It can be parking your car further away in the parking lot at work, or the grocery store, or at church on Sundays. Parking further away could reduce stress levels alone because we wouldn't be hunting for the best spot where someone cuts right in front of us from the other direction and peels into the "perfect spot" we are obviously heading towards WITH OUR TURN INDICATOR ON (Ok, I can't be the only one this has happened to! Don't be that person, ladies. Don't be that person!) Or, perhaps take a walk around the block when we go out to get the mail instead of just walking to the mailbox.

If you are currently pregnant, it may be helpful to know what The American College of Obstetricians and Gynecologists say about pregnancy and working out. Their website states that experts agree the following exercises are safest for pregnant women:

* Walking—Brisk walking provides a total body workout and is easy on the joints and muscles.
* Swimming and water workouts—Water workouts use many of the body's muscles. The water supports your weight so you avoid injury and muscle strain.
* Stationary bicycling—Because your growing belly can affect your balance and make you more prone to falls, riding a standard bicycle during pregnancy can be risky. Cycling on a stationary bike is a better choice.
* Modified yoga and modified Pilates—Yoga reduces

stress, improves flexibility, and encourages stretching and focused breathing. There are prenatal yoga and Pilates classes designed for pregnant women. These classes often teach modified poses which accommodate a pregnant woman's shifting balance. You should avoid poses that require you to be still or lie on your back for long periods.[15]

If you are an experienced runner, jogger, or racquet-sports player, you may be able to keep doing these activities during pregnancy. Discuss these options with your ob-gyn.

There are so many free pregnancy workouts available on YouTube. Just be sure to vet the trainer and listen to your body. If something doesn't feel like it is agreeing with you that day, it doesn't mean it won't work for the rest of your pregnancy. Each of my pregnancies were different in their own right. I continued running with my son until I was six months pregnant, but the belly wasn't the reason I stopped. I was running one Saturday morning, on the precise Saturday morning the annual, community-wide yard sale took place. While window shopping, well I guess "run-by-front-lawn shopping," I got distracted. I tripped on the sidewalk and nearly went down. Out of pure shock, I screamed loud enough that everyone within a block turned to see the commotion. Since he was my first, and my belly wasn't really protruding an incredible amount, I hollered, "Don't worry! I'm fine! I'm just six months pregnant!" Not sure if that eased the tension or made it worse, but I briskly walked away like a speed walker in the Olympics.

Whatever you do, start small and count the victories. I've found it is easier to make good choices for the rest of the day if I start off with a good choice for my body. It's almost as if I don't want to eat the extra dessert or drink the juice because I don't want to undo the good I've already done. You would think it would work the opposite. "Well, I worked out today, so I can cheat a little here and there." But for me it is the exact opposite. Working out makes my self-discipline muscles stronger. I hope you find this to be true for yourself as well.

It would be a complete miss for me to leave out the spiritual component of keeping our bodies healthy. Whether you see your body as sheer perfection or not, your body is an image bearer of Christ. The Bible explains it this way, saying, "Do you not know that your bodies are temples of the Holy Spirit, who is in you, whom you have received from God? You are not your own; you were bought at a price. Therefore honor God with your bodies" (1 Corinthians 6:19-20).

What exactly was this price? How much are we really worth? Well, let me start by explaining how God spared no expense in making a free gift available to each of us, His beloved children. If this gift has not been presented to you, please let me have the honor of telling you it is for you. God is for you. God created us as relational beings. After creating Adam, the Lord said, "It is not good for the man to be alone. I will make a helper suitable for him." He paraded all the existing animals and birds on Earth and let Adam name each one of them, but as God knew would happen, Adam found no suitable partner. The Lord then created Eve. Adam knew instantly she was special and set apart from all other creatures. She was his soulmate (Genesis 2:18-23). The world was not right for Adam without Eve. The Lord created us to be in relationship with one another and in relationship with him. But, sin, aka death, entered the world through Eve and Adam's choice to exercise free will and eat from the Tree of Knowledge of Good and Evil.

Adam and Eve are not alone in sin. Romans 3:23 says we have ALL fallen short of the glory of God. Another way to explain this is that we all have a Jesus-shaped hole in our hearts which we tirelessly try to fill. We show this constant struggle through our pursuit of things like relationships, grades in school or promotions at work, fashion, body image, perfection for approval, wealth, the right house, prescription drugs, street drugs or alcohol, all trying to reach our fleshly desire to have a full life. Romans 6:23 explains the penalty for sin is death. God did the priceless, hard work of sending Jesus, His only son to Earth, to live the perfect life we could never bear, so that when Jesus Christ died, He paid this penalty for all past, current, and future sins on the Earth (Romans 5:8). Jesus came to make forgiveness and salvation possible. He took on Himself the judgment we deserve. He canceled our debt record. Wiped it clean. Fresh start! Our only role now is to make our own choice of free will. We serve a loving God who allows us the freedom of choice. We can choose to be forgiven for our sin and receive the gift of eternal life. But like any gift, it becomes ours only when we respond and receive it. Faith is an essential part of salvation. There are many kinds of beliefs and faith, but not all are linked to salvation. I may say I believe a chair will hold my weight. But, I only really believe it when I commit myself and sit down. The faith of salvation involves an act of commitment and trust, in which you commit your life to Jesus Christ and trust Him alone as your Savior and Lord.

Although we've already spent eight weeks together inviting the Lord to work in our lives, I don't want to assume that every one of you has taken the most important step in your role as a daughter of Christ herself. Committing your life to Jesus is a personal and individual decision. By praying a prayer like this, you are inviting Jesus into your life and releasing your cares and worries to Him.

> *"Jesus, right now, I ask You to become Lord of my life. You are my Savior and I thank You for the sacrifice You made on the cross. I receive Your grace and confidently believe my life is forever changed.*
>
> *Jesus, help me to live for You. My heart and my life are open to what You have for me. I want to know Your ways and love people as You love me. Thank You for Your mercy, hope, and unfailing love.*
>
> *In Your name I pray, Amen."*

If you've just prayed this prayer of salvation, we'd love to celebrate with you! Let us know about your decision for Jesus by scanning the QR Code below and filling out the form. We want to help you with your next steps on your faith journey.

➡️ **Jump to pages 46-50 in the Full Hands, Full Life Activity Companion Guide for this week's interactive prompts.**

Week 9: Serving Others

Here we go again. A topic that may send you running for the hills. Kudos to you for sticking with this journey and nearing the end of quarter one. My hope is that these past eight weeks have helped you establish some new rhythms in your life that are serving you well while bringing you clarity in your relationship with the Lord and His plan for your life. Well, serving others is no different. It is all about perspective.

In the Summer of 2015, while expecting our fourth child—our third little girl—our sweet friends and family wanted to throw us a baby shower. How generous!

But something about it just didn't seem right.

See, I'd already been blessed by family and friends during our last three pregnancies, yet expecting moms in the community didn't have the first diaper or clean onesie to welcome home their little blessing.

Well, the Holy Spirit works in mysterious ways. With this internal struggle going on, I ran out to pick the girls up from preschool. The radio station, still tuned to 88.3 from the movie they watched in the car the night before, typically brought in straight static, but this hot summer day, it brought the signal through clear as day.

A published author and talk show host shared how she involved her children in small acts of kindness to help instill in them the beauty of a servant's heart. One idea she posed was hosting a community baby shower. Everyone likes buying for babies—right?

I felt the undeniable nudge (well, shove) to throw my baby shower for a local non-profit instead. The invite list grew from a few close family and friends to hundreds of women in the community.

From the outpouring of donations benefiting one of our partnering non-profits, I saw the generosity of the hearts of the women of our local community as tables were filled with thousands of diapers, hundreds of wipes, tons of outfits, brand new cribs, and car seats. This quickly grew to an annual event where 30,000+ items were being donated.

The reality is women within walking distance of our own homes, in rooms down the hall at work or school, and even in our closest circle of friends are in need of restoration.

Being born as "heirs to the throne of Christ" (Romans 8:17), we are all royal in His eyes. We can trust each other for support and lift one another up by extending grace and blessing one another one kind act at a time. Whether it be time, energy, prayer, resources, or talents, we all have a variety of blessings to offer our community during every phase of our lives. The struggle is finding where and figuring out how we can make the most impact when the timing is right.

This initial nudge from the Holy Spirit to give back to ladies in the local community turned into founding a 501c-3 non-profit organization, Her Community, Inc., dedicated to helping women bloom where they've been planted. After several years, the Community Baby Shower grew into a year-round Blessings Closet, helping supply essential baby items for teen moms involved in our local mentor program, but I didn't want our impact to stop with transactional giving. I wanted to provide more opportunities for the women receiving blessings to connect with the women providing the support. In my experience, a large difference in impact exists between transactional giving and transformational blessings for both parties involved—the recipient and the sower. As a mother of many littles, I personally knew how volunteering for even just a few hours fueled me up to serve my family better when I walked back through our door. Our HER board members believed in this so much that we initiated a childcare reimbursement policy for moms hiring sitters to watch their littles in order to exercise their servant hearts outside of the home.

What started as a transactional giving effort morphed into transformational serving through a Christmas blessing initiative. We strategically connected local businesses, churches, and friend groups with single mothers in their local neighborhood unable to provide Christmas for their children. These mothers, whose need and gift requests were vetted by another local non-profit, would meet volunteers from the community in which they lived at a Christmas wrapping party. Christmas music filled the air. Overflowing spreads of refreshments lined the counters, and tables spilled over with the thousands of clothes, toys, shoes, books and hygiene items hand selected by the community volunteers for each individual mother.

While tinsel fell to the floor and scissors sliced through festive wrapping paper, my favorite part of the experience came from listening to the conversations happening around the tables. Previously shattered dreams becoming alive once again. One particular year, the Holy Spirit divinely led one mother to be paired with a volunteer who worked in higher education. This mother had stopped pursuing her dream of working in healthcare after she found out she had an aggressive form of cancer. Expensive treatments cost her and her teenage son their home and livelihood. Not only had her desire to continue education stopped, but her desire to live was in jeopardy. Through these tabletop conversations she not only regained her faith in her ability to see beyond her circumstances, but also regained faith that her purpose in life was not over. The volunteer got in her corner, championed her re-enrollment process, and became her cheerleader. An anonymous donor supplied a brand new laptop for schoolwork. Since the wrapping party, by the grace of God, this single mom has been pronounced cancer free, finished her degree, and now works in healthcare helping restore other cancer patient's belief in not taking any of life's moments for granted but instead making every moment count. Transformational giving is only possible when we put our "yes" on the table to serve others around us.

Giving back does not have to be financially, and it doesn't have to be across town. Sometimes giving your time, energy, and prayers are more sacrificial than a monetary donation. 1 Peter 4:10-11 urges us into serving by saying, "Each of you should use whatever gift you have received to serve others, as faithful stewards of God's grace in its various forms. Do not be slothful in zeal, be fervent in spirit, serve the Lord."

We all embody a way we can bless others. If you are pregnant, have an infant at home, or are in the midst of job or housing insecurity, it might not feel like you have the bandwidth to give back. I understand. It reminds me of when a busy single person talks about how they will never have time for a relationship. Then they meet someone they can't imagine spending time without. The look of their weekly schedule suddenly has pockets of hours they spend with this person. Chris and I sometimes ponder the question, "What did we do with all our time before kids came along?" We had a solid two years of marriage before Brooks was born, but in the blink of an eye, all that time we probably wasted felt purposeful and driven.

This week, seek out a place where you can give back in your community. The specific way you serve is not the most important piece. Get out of your comfort zone, but stay within your skillset and help someone in need. Then evaluate the feelings you have about the experience to see if you believe that opportunity aligned with your gifting.

Here are a few ideas to help brainstorm:

Is there a local pregnancy resource center in your area?
* Donate any baby items you've received, new or gently used that you don't have a need for.

* Offer to help sort donated items for them if time permits. These items help expectant mothers welcome their babies home with the items needed to keep them safe, warm, and fed.

Are you part of a local church?
* Offer to serve in the children's ministry one Sunday a month. If you are a new mom, or mom-to-be, this can be a place where you can serve with your baby or practice caring for babies with loving volunteers by your side.

* Volunteer on the creative arts or greeting team. Roles like running a camera or holding doors open with a smile are valuable roles typically filled by volunteers each weekend.

Do you enjoy cooking?
* Bless a friend or family member with a home-cooked meal, perhaps someone going through a tough season or recovering from illness. For some meals that are easy to double, I'll make enough to surprise someone with an unannounced meal delivered on their doorstep.

* Host a dinner at your home and invite a neighbor who will be shocked to receive the invitation.

Although serving can drain you of energy, there is a deep sense of peace and belonging when you find the capacity to serve that aligns with the God-given purpose He has in your life.

➡️ **Jump to pages 52-56 in the Full Hands, Full Life Activity Companion Guide for this week's interactive prompts.**

Week 10: Defining your Destiny/ Personal Transformation

Ever heard the phrase, "she comes by it naturally"? Have others used that phrase to explain one of your attributes? Have you said it to excuse the actions of those around you? Have you used that phrase as a cop out for your own character trait?

The phrase itself holds some weight of truth, but the truth behind it does not have to define our future. We all possess not only the ability, but also the desire to grow beyond our circumstances. For decades, I used this phrase to explain lashing out with brash remarks, delivering truths with a less than graceful tone, and defending myself when I took a blow to my ego. By the grace of God, I'm coming to grips with the truth that these interactions all lead me to shame. They don't even feel healthy in the moment. They feel wrong. Unwarranted.

I don't know about you, but my inner dialogue can be downright nasty. Not necessarily towards others, but I'm definitely judgmental of myself. If not kept in check, I can start spiraling down the mental battlefield of perfection and productivity.

Join me on a typical mental spiral journey: *"Wow, that went really poorly! Should I have done things differently? Gosh, I really blew it. That person will never trust me again. How could I be so naive?"*

When it comes to productivity, my unchecked, inner dialogue goes something like this: *"I'm already behind on what I needed to get done today. What still needs to be done? I should have already completed XYZ by this point in the day/week/month/year/life. Why even bother with doing it now? What difference will it make? Today was a failure. I'm a failure."*

The dangers of mental spiraling are never more glaring than when interrupted by interactions with others. When one of my half dozen angels walked up to me one morning to ask me a simple question, "What's for dinner?" she never anticipated the response: "I can't believe you are asking me about dinner? It isn't even lunchtime yet! Do you even remember a time when I didn't put something on a plate for you? Do you really think today is the first day in your entire life when I'd force you to fend for yourself!"

Sadly, this isn't a hypothetical conversation. It was an actual response I gave to one of my daughters who has a particular interest in knowing what meals to expect throughout the day. It wasn't her specific question that caused the eruption; it was the forty-seven other questions I was consecutively shaming myself with internally which overwhelmed my ability to respond maturely.

This interaction gave me a launching point. I placed a stake in the ground of correcting this character flaw when I saw the expression in her eyes shift from a playful, jovial inquiry to confusion mixed with fear.

Since the question "What's for dinner?" stressed me

out that much, I made a hard copy meal plan for the week so she and I could reference it together as many times a day as our hearts desired. My response that particular day brought along a truckload of remorse. Something had to shift, and that something had to start on the battlefield in my mind.

Maybe there is a space in your life where you feel this type of heavy shame. If so, let me share how the Holy Spirit used a devotion on Colossians 3:15 to convict my heart in the most gentle way. I hope this lands softly on your heart, providing clarity for you as well.

"Put on then, as God's chosen ones, holy and beloved, compassionate hearts, kindness, humility, meekness, and patience . . ."
Colossians 3:12 (ESV)

My blaring outbursts felt wrong because I was putting on clothing the Lord did not intend for me to wear. Becoming a softer, more compassionate, and kinder person initially felt like selling out. Would those who knew me before even recognize a humble, meek, or patient person? At that time, I couldn't fathom someone striving to be described as meek, and humility sounded like a coward's answer for not sticking up for themselves. However, this couldn't be further from the truth. The more I leaned into the Holy Spirit's guidance on how to interact with others while extending grace to myself, the more I began to feel a peaceful, humble confidence. I was growing into the Meredith the Lord created me to be and less like the Meredith the world pushed me into being.

Standing up and being different from what is around you takes mental fortitude mixed with brave determination. Thankfully an example of complete, unashamed life transformation shows up in the life of a very unexpected man in history. Paul, formerly called Saul, lived during Jesus's lifetime. Employed as a judge in the Judean court, Paul approved the execution of a follower of Jesus. Paul's ruling of Stephen, a man arrested for proclaiming the good news of Jesus and healing people in his name (Acts 8:1), spread throughout the city. Paul quickly gained notoriety and power. Citizens of Jerusalem laid their cloaks, their most prized article of clothing, at Paul's feet during this trial showing their allegiance to the court and the weight Paul's decision held on the future of society.

Paul had skin in the game. His reputation, financial security, and purpose in life became synonymous with his goal to eradicate Christianity from the face of the Earth. As a friend of people in high standing and a member of the upper class, Paul's life was held in the balance.

Spoiler alert: Paul becomes arguably the most influential person in the Christian faith, writing half of the books in the New Testament.

In Galatians, which is a New Testament letter from Paul to the people of Galatia, he self-described his role in the judicial system by saying, "For you have heard of my previous way of life in Judaism, how intensely I persecuted the church of God and tried to destroy it. I was advancing in Judaism beyond many of my own age among my people and was extremely zealous for the traditions of my fathers" (Galatians 1:13-14).

So, what caused his radical shift in convictions? Paul, previously Saul, described his divine encounter in Acts 9. On the road to Damascus, a trip to arrest Christians in that area, "suddenly a light from heaven flashed around him. He fell to the ground and heard a voice say to him, 'Saul, Saul, why do you persecute me?'

'Who are you, Lord?' Saul asked.

'I am Jesus, whom you are persecuting,' he replied. 'Now get up and go into the city, and you will be told what you must do'" (Acts 9:3-9).

The men traveling with Saul stood there speechless; they heard the sound but did not see anyone. Paul got up from the ground, but when he opened his eyes, he could see nothing. So they led him by the hand into Damascus. For three days, he was blind and did not eat or drink anything.

Simultaneously, an angel appeared to an unlikely citizen, Ananias of Damascus, instructing him to go find Paul in Judas's house on a street called Straight (I absolutely love this detail because Jesus makes Paul's path in life straight on a street called Straight!) and restored his sight. Initially, Ananias was respectfully reluctant. I imagine he was thinking, *"Do what? You want me to go find this man who is persecuting, arresting, and killing these brothers of mine; breaking up families; and leaving a trail of broken homes behind, all for the sake of the same beliefs in Jesus that I believe? Sounds more like a personal death sentence for me. Hard pass, Jesus."*

But Ananias obeyed this divine appointment.

"Ananias went to the house and entered it. Placing his hands on Saul, he said, 'Brother Saul, the Lord—Jesus, who appeared to you on the road as you were coming here—has sent me so that you may see again and be filled with the Holy Spirit.' Immediately, something like scales fell from Saul's eyes, and he could see again. He got up and was baptized, and after taking some food, he regained his strength."
Acts 9:13-19

You can read the detailed account of this encounter in Acts 9, again in summary form in Acts 22, and a further condensed acknowledgement of the event's impact in 2 Corinthians 10.

Paul, well-known and praised for his intense persecution of the followers of Jesus, started sharing the good news immediately. He believed.

I'm so thankful God put Paul's transformation on full display in the Bible. What this story communicates to me is we are never too lost from our intended purpose or too far down the wrong path in life. There is no number of wrong actions that disqualify us in God's eyes. After the healing, Paul immediately got up and was baptized. God turned Paul's spirit of conviction in the right direction. A wise mentor of mine once told me "a strong-willed, stubborn child is only a challenge when they are not taught how to harness that will in the right direction." Such power exists in this belief!

God turned Paul's weak spot—his unwavering convictions—into his strongest ally. His profession kept him in the crossbows of danger, yet his bravery let him walk through and navigate the courts time and time again to share his testimony with previous co-workers, friends, bosses, and even family. With unwavering faith, he was kidnapped (Acts 21:27), beaten (Acts 21:30-31; 23:3), threatened (Acts 22:22; 27:42), arrested many times (Acts 21:33; 22:24, 31; 23:35; 28:16), accused in lawsuits (Acts 21:34; 22:30; 24:1-2; 25:2, 7; 28:4), interrogated (Acts 25:24-27), ridiculed (Acts 26:24), ignored (Acts 27:11), shipwrecked (Acts 27:41), and bitten by a viper (Acts 28:3) all for the sake of spreading the good news of the gospel he previously loathed.

I don't have the luxury of knowing your story—the intricate details which led you to read these words today—but God does. Chance did not lead you to spend these moments reading the truth. The power to grow beyond the cards of life you have been dealt or the choices you've made exists. Perhaps some of these life choices were made for you. Maybe you innocently started out on a path that ended up leading you to a darker place than you ever dared to imagine. Paul faced many worldly temptations—fame, power, money, security, protection. His road led to a very dark place, where he found comfort in the abyss. But this same Paul attests to the truth that, "The temptations in your life are no different from what others experience. And God is faithful. He will not allow the temptation to be more than you can stand. When you are tempted, he will show you a way out so you can endure" (1 Corinthians 10:13, NLT).

Have faith to stand on that promise. The Lord will provide a pathway out of whatever worldly temptations you find yourself in. Seek the light, a way out, and an uncharted path in the other direction.

➡️ **Jump to pages 58-62 in the Full Hands, Full Life Activity Companion Guide for this week's interactive prompts.**

Weeks 11-20
Battling Mindsets

Full Hands, Full Life

Week 11: Negativity / Power of Words

Welcome to quarter two of this journey together. If we found ourselves as teammates on a field, the second quarter means our nerves are a bit more settled. We know what our opponents brought to the field. Perhaps the scoreboard reflects we took the field and dominated play, which brings a new confidence to the team. Maybe the other team came out to play from the start and we found ourselves trailing, which gives us extra fire in our team huddle declaring we didn't show up to let them make a spectacle of us. Take a moment to think through your quarter one of this journey and give us a score. Yes, I say us because I am in this with you. I've been praying for you along this journey and want you to experience the winning feeling of freedom at the end more than you, perhaps, even want it for yourself! Now, let's get back on the field and show our opponents—the enemy, patterns of this world, and life circumstances beyond our control—whose team we are on and what we are fighting for!

During quarter one, we worked on establishing rhythms in our daily life—habits and actions which promise growth. If observed by an outsider, they could pinpoint new routines that, ten weeks ago, were absent from our days. This quarter, we turn our attention inward, battling mindsets that thrive in the depths of our soul. An onlooker may never see the change taking place, but the way we interact with ourselves and others will reap the benefits of these next ten weeks. So, let's dive in.

When was the last time someone spoke words to you that cut to the core? Notice I didn't ask if it has happened, but when. Words can hurt. The sting can last far longer than physical pain—a day, a week, a month, a lifetime. We all seek approval from others in one way or another. We may even sacrifice a part of ourselves along the way in hopes of gaining acceptance, love, and a sense of belonging, and those closest to us gain space in our life to say things that cut the deepest.

Before we started our homeschooling journey, our children attended a wonderful Christian, private school in town where I taught for several years. As our oldest daughter, Ellie, was in her early years in elementary school, she had a teacher who loved her students fiercely and earned their admiration and love back. She was not the soft-spoken, endearing type of teacher who may come to mind, but instead held a high standard for each student paired with tough love.

Ellie is my right-hand assistant and has been since day one—cooking, cleaning, organizing, and babysitting. Once, while leaving for a work trip, Chris asked me to make sure to let Ellie know that she didn't have to try to be me while I was gone—he could handle it too. Although I didn't set up that expectation with Ellie, she assumed the role and found success in it. When Ellie was only sixteen months old, her first little sister, Leighton, was born, and Ellie immediately started helping care for the baby as much as her little hands and legs could manage. This desire to help everyone, paired with her unique passion for organization and time management, makes her such a gift to me as a mom of many. My answer to the question, "How do you get it all done?" is many times, "It wouldn't have happened without Ellie!"

Now, during this particular year of elementary school, Ellie was already excelling in dance at such a high level that she had 10-12 hours of rehearsals split over four nights of the week. Her school days started in "before school care" and ended in "after school care" so I could finish my teacher duties each day. She was also involved in other extracurriculars like piano and basketball, and to top it all off, we were still adjusting to adding her third baby sister into our world. Yet, she managed to enjoy taking on responsibilities of caring for her little sisters and loving the newest baby, but I have to admit it was one of the hardest years for me as a mom. I was using all my energy and patience up on others, leaving the worst for my own family. In the mornings, I was barking at them to get out the door or we would be late. As I found them all over campus in afterschool areas, I was rushing them away from their friends and saying things like, "No, you're gonna have to hold it till we get there because we are already late!" Bedtime routines didn't include songs and stories from their days. I counted it a win when they were all in bed with prayers said and no tears shed. Basically, I was a people shuffler and not a child nurturer. Papers came home that didn't get signed, last minute class party shopping meant our plans for fun crafty snacks got thrown out the window, and week long projects turned into Thursday night cram sessions where we traded off tears. For Ellie, this burden of being unprepared was heavy.

On one particular night, Ellie climbed up in my bed after all the littles were down for us to have a talk. She was more somber than usual. I asked how school was and the tears started flowing. She started with, "Remember those papers for the field trip?" A lightbulb came on and I said, "Oh, yeah! We need to get those in." And, she said, "Needed, Mom. They were due today, and everyone else had theirs."

My heart sank. Ellie had given them to me with plenty of time; I just failed to take the time to fill them out. As the teacher noticed that Ellie didn't turn hers in, she commented,

"You are so unorganized, I'm surprised you can keep your head on straight! I can only imagine what your room is like at home." She continued on to mention something about whether I, as her mother, allowed her to be so unorganized at home and then alluded to it probably being how many kids we have that made it impossible to keep anything in order. The worst part was, she said this to Ellie in front of the entire class. Ellie's little organized, help everyone, team player heart was crushed, and my momma bear heart was enraged. How dare someone make a spectacle of my child in front of everyone on something that was my own fault to begin with? At that moment, I was able to talk with Ellie about how brave she was to share this with me. We discussed how making a point of someone else in front of others is unkind and her feelings were warranted. I apologized for my part in this happening, promised to do my part to make it right, and explained how much of a gift she is to me and our family in the exact skill set that her teacher said she was lacking. Her teacher could not have been more wrong on her assumptions.

I'm the first to admit I struggle with taking offense. The teacher's comments felt like a dagger as I felt judgment on my ability to manage a family of our size. Chris and I have always felt passionate that our kids did not choose to be born into a large family. They are unique image bearers of Christ who should be given the opportunity to explore their God-given talents as if they were only children.

After sleeping on it and cooling off a bit, I went in to talk with the teacher—signed paper and cash in hand. As teachers, you never truly know what battles your students have already been through or are escaping from as they walk through your door. To use one student to make a point to all the others may help the majority in the short run, but it crushes the spirit of one along the way.

As expected, the teacher didn't remember the comments she made in passing that Ellie recited with clarity. She didn't mean to label Ellie as unorganized and messy. She didn't mean to question our parenting ability.

She wholeheartedly apologized, but the thing about words is that you can't take them back. We get to choose the words we say and how we say them, but we don't get to choose how they are received by others. That is why the Bible speaks with such clarity on the power of the tongue.

Proverbs 18:20-21 states, "From the fruit of their mouth a person's stomach is filled; with the harvest of their lips they are satisfied. The tongue has the power of life and death, and those who love it will eat its fruit." Notice this states that both life and death can be spoken from the same mouth.

The beauty in the power of words is that positive affirmations hold just as much strength as negative ones. We get the choice of words. Matthew 15:11 takes this a step further and says, "It is not what goes into the mouth that defiles a person, but what comes out of the mouth; this defiles a person." What we choose to eat and drink doesn't ultimately make us clean or dirty, but the words we speak over ourselves and others is what changes our cleanliness.

Thankfully Ellie confided in me so I could speak affirmations over her that evening. The truths I shared sank in deep and skimmed the other comments from the surface. I've only seen her love for organization, time management, and helping her siblings soar. However, when people of authority assign you a label, they tend to stick.

It is important to continually affirm the positive character traits and growing gifts in our children so our voices will be what they hear when others poke holes of doubt in them. If you see your child makes friends easily, praise them for being so welcoming and having such a gift for including others instead of making passing comments of "He never knows a stranger" or "She could talk to a wall." If you see your child notices when you are sad or stressed, praise them for having such empathy and compassion for others; don't shame them for trying to pry into your business. You can gently explain it's something you aren't ready to share with them yet, but you are impressed with how in-tune they are with others' emotions.

The character traits the Lord crafted into your children will ring loudest. When we find ways to steer them into positively using those attributes, it helps create pathways to successful futures in line with the plan the Lord has in store for them.

What labels have others put on you? Type A? Inconsistent? Easy? Push over? Unworthy? Are you choosing to speak affirmations of life or death over your circumstances, your health, your finances, your relationships? Start taking mental stock of what you are thinking. This week's journaling space encourages you to write down and capture your thoughts. If they are negative, that's okay! Start with writing down those negative thoughts and write a positive one next to them.

➡️ **Jump to pages 64-68 in the
Full Hands, Full Life Activity Companion Guide
for this week's interactive prompts.**

Week 12: Unexpected / Failure

When you first found out you were pregnant, did you start imagining what your baby would look like? Were you terrified, relieved, or happy? Were you seeing yourself drawn to either baby girl clothes or baby boy clothes in the stores?

When I found out I was pregnant, I imagined being a #boymom. I pictured a gaggle of boys in my van with all the dirt and smells that comes with it. True to my thoughts, our first was a boy. I was over the moon with my little prince. When we found out we were expecting our second, I immediately jumped into how fun it would be for Brooks and his brother to play ball together in the backyard, go camping and fishing with each other, and have hiking buddies for myself. I even went so far as to dream of having Brooks with multiple brothers standing in front of the "Brooks' Brothers" clothing store window at the mall. What a picture that would be some day!

At sixteen weeks pregnant with our second child, I caught the norovirus. Unlike catching a foul ball, catching this virus took me out! When you've been vomiting on repeat for seven hours straight, the mind plays crazy tricks on you in the middle of the night. Since Brooks was still a baby and his sleep routine held utmost importance to us, I decided the only option was for me to drive myself to the local hospital in between trips to the bathroom while my husband stayed home with him. I was worried about the growing baby since I was only sixteen weeks pregnant and wasn't feeling the baby very frequently. What if I had become too dehydrated? How would I know if the violent vomiting had jostled the baby from the placenta?

Much like contractions, I started timing my bathroom visits. I realized I was on a 14-minute cycle. That meant if I got my purse and shoes on in one break and then drove to the hospital eight minutes away during the next break I would be able to park the car and make it into the ER before the urge to throw up my insides came on again. I made it into triage just in time to ask for a bag followed quickly by medication that pushed the brakes on my tummy crisis.

Side note—bless the hearts of the ER triage nurses! They never know what to expect in their shifts, but just to expect the unexpected. Life becomes certain of the uncertain and requires the ability to adjust and thrive in that state of chaos. They are examples of Jesus drawing near to those others go out of their way to avoid.

In triage, I learned that I was two weeks shy of the cutoff to be sent straight to the mother/baby unit for monitoring, so I had to stay in the ER and wait for a bed. They came to get me and wheeled me into the ultrasound room to check on the baby. I was relieved to see the little baby wiggling around but had trouble watching the screen during the waves of nausea. It was there, in the cold, sterile room in the middle of the night that I learned, alone, with the glazed doughnut sweaty look from nausea, that I was having a little girl.

Immediately, I felt unequipped to be a girl mom. The weight of knowing what I put my parents through during the teenage years, which was only a fraction of the whole picture, was overwhelming. I wasn't honest with them and was terrified at having a level of secrecy between me and my daughters. I felt more equipped to help boys learn how to treat a lady, how to look for markers of a good wife, and how to let chivalry be a lamppost for manhood. When it came to raising Godly women who would treat their bodies as temples of the Holy Spirit, that was completely out of the realm of possibility for me.

But, God has a plan bigger than we can imagine. Not only was I gifted our first daughter to shepherd into womanhood, the Lord saw fit to bless me with five daughters to help raise up into the calling the Lord has on their lives.

Perhaps your pregnancy was unexpected. Perhaps in the eyes of others, or even your own, the baby is a mistake. From the hospital bed that dark, lonely night, I experienced similar thoughts. I felt scared, and if I'm honest, a bit disappointed, the Lord made a mistake giving me a baby girl. How could He want me to be the example for her to follow since He knew all my mistakes and failures inside and out? I hadn't led a life worthy of having daughters. But God's plan is always greater.

As my good friend Megan shares with all the moms in our mentor program, "How you see this baby, as a blessing or a burden, will shape how you interact with him or her." I chose to see my baby girl as a blessing, and it has made all the difference.

In Isaiah 61, the prophet Isaiah says, "The Spirit of the Sovereign Lord is on me, because the Lord has appointed me to preach good news to the poor. He has sent me to bind up the brokenhearted, to proclaim freedom for the captives and release from darkness for the prisoners... to bestow on them a crown of beauty instead of ashes, the oil of gladness instead of mourning, and a garment of praise instead of a spirit of despair. They will be called oaks of righteousness, a planting of the Lord for the display of his splendor."

My life prior to motherhood was riddled with relational ashes. My mental fortitude and value as a woman was founded in all the wrong places. I exploited attributes to gain advantages and truly thought I was a master chess player in life when in actuality I was just a pawn being played. Teaching our daughters about modesty and messages we are sending in public has been incredibly humbling. Helping establish a firm foundation on where their value lies reestablished mine. My opportunity to help teach and lead my daughters into being oaks of righteousness for the display of his splendor is a gift—one I do not take lightly.

This counter cultural perspective on being a woman is tough. Our need for beauty to come from ashes is because life can be riddled with heartache. If beauty can't come from ashes then why invest in relationships with others, start a new job, or dream of good things for our futures? Don't all these have the potential to be thrown into the fire of life simply leaving ashes behind? The Lord promises to bestow a crown of beauty instead of ashes on the poor and brokenhearted. Through the redemptive blood of Jesus, my view of beauty has been restored. As Jesus preached in the synagogue in Nazareth, He used these verses from Isaiah mentioned previously to explain that His purpose in coming to Earth was to proclaim freedom for the prisoners and release the oppressed. He is still in the business of doing just that. He took my heart, held captive in how the world viewed me, and set me free by how He views me—a redeemed daughter of the Most High King, planted right here in this life of a mom of six to display His cleansing power.

The Lord promises to bring beauty out of ashes, so let Him start forming your crown of beauty today.

➡ Jump to pages 70-74 in the
Full Hands, Full Life Activity Companion Guide
for this week's interactive prompts.

Week 13: Anxiety

On January 1, 2020, no one made their New Year's resolution to build resilience through a global pandemic. Alas, that resolution became a shared goal worldwide. On March 11, 2020, I remember curling up on the couch to watch the third period of an NHL hockey game when Chris read out a tweet that the NBA suspended its 2019-2020 season "until further notice." We were shocked. Over the next twenty-four hours we watched in disbelief as the MLS, NFL, MLB, NHL, NASCAR, and even Formula 1 all postponed current seasons and training camps. Keep in mind March holds the most revenue for many of these sports as they enter the playoffs and post season with peak ticket prices and concessions.

Being small business owners, Chris and I felt the challenges of a global shutdown on a raw, personal level. Our business, Liquid 5th, specializes in live sound and album production of a cappella music. A cappella groups perform by singing without instrumental accompaniment—all voices; no instruments. The intricacy of this style of music hinges on the close proximity of its group members to one another. Social distancing put a full stop on live performances and the creation of the musical form as a whole. Within a two-week period, we lost 100% of our live shows and album recordings for the next 12 months. Revenue plummeted. Calendar wiped clean.

As a wife, I wanted to emotionally support my husband. As a mom, I desired to shield our kids from the uncertainty of our future. As a business owner, I felt the weight of keeping a stream of revenue to make payroll for our team of employees, who all felt like family.

The truth of spring 2020 is we saw our livelihood held in the balance. This perfect storm brought on a wave of anxiety I've never experienced before. While I wrote these words, my heart rate started picking up and my eyes welled up with tears. Perhaps you've experienced this type of heavy burden. Everything feels like it depends on you to keep control, move forward, and find solutions. Except the more you try to solve the problems, the clearer the reality becomes that the control is completely out of your hands.

One morning I could no longer hide the anxiety I was experiencing. I woke up and my eyes had nearly swollen shut. My face puffed up to the point of being unrecognizable. My fluid-filled cheeks held the pin-prickling feeling you experience after your foot falls asleep. During my telehealth visit with a doctor, without hesitation I could state that nothing in my diet had changed and no new facial regimens were introduced because we were on complete lockdown. Everything I had eaten came from my kitchen. Shipments had stopped arriving at the front step. My diagnosis: extreme, stress-induced inflammation.

My deep dive into home anxiety remedies took off. I combed through research studies. I read self-help books. I knew the inward discomfort I experienced would show up physically again and again if I didn't fight for clarity. My biggest concern was that this mental battle would become contagious to my children. Children look up to their caretakers, for better or for worse. They emulate the patterns and behaviors around them. If I could no longer hide the anxious thoughts taking residence in my mind, then it was time to give them an eviction notice.

What I found true for me is the battle against anxiety is fought in the mind. The beauty is that it is right where we are, right now. No need to go searching to find it. The unpleasant truth is that we can't easily run from it. We have to battle through it. We have to become victorious over the anxious thoughts.

Growing up in the 80s and 90s, anxiety and mental health weren't tabletop discussion points. Chatting with friends, the topic never breached the conversation. After the first year of Covid, the World Health Institute put out a brief which explained that anxiety and depression saw a massive 25% increase worldwide.16 Youth and women showed to be affected the worst. Some reassurance comes to mind when you know you are not alone in your struggles. There are others out there struggling through this isolating, introspective fight. Please let me acknowledge there are mental health diagnoses that warrant the use of medication, and this next section is not trying to undermine the medical sector and its importance in mental health. Those types of medical conditions were not what I was experiencing. My prayer is that by sharing the following ways I battled and found freedom from anxiety will help you become victorious in your journey if it resembles mine.

Out of all the podcasts, research studies, and self-help books I devoured, the Holy Spirit showed up loudest in scripture. When I read through verses familiar to me, I uncovered truths previously undiscovered when I began asking myself these questions:

Who are we fighting?

The devil, often referred to as the thief in the Bible, "comes only to steal and kill and destroy" (John 10:10a). My contentment and security was being placed in all the wrong things! I realized that by viewing my circumstances from a worldly perspective, I was allowing the devil to sneak in and steal my inner peace, replacing it with anxiety.

Ephesians 6, one of my absolute favorite chapters in all the Bible declares, "For our struggle is not against flesh and blood, but against the rulers, against the authorities, against the powers of this dark world and against the spiritual forces of evil in the heavenly realms." As much as I wanted to blame others for my sadness, my feelings of helplessness, or my isolation, it wasn't people that were out to get me. It was the devil taking full advantage of the current state of the world and capitalizing on my vulnerability. He was putting his spiritual army into battle formation, and I was just trying to turn around and run. It was time to armor up!

What are the steps to become victorious in the moment?

All battle fronts have their lookout points; perhaps a tall tower with guards stationed to survey the landscape twenty-four hours a day. In today's society, military reconnaissance–an operation to obtain information relating to the activities, resources, or military forces–implores balloons, aviation, and space technology round the clock to detect aggressive advances. I needed to find my internal reconnaissance. I quickly identified my chest tightening and feeling a lump in the back of my throat as warning signs. The same physical manifestations that once caused my mind to say, "no, no, no… it's happening again!" became a gift from the Lord. I could catch the anxiety attack before it settled in too deep.

Without delay, I began taking a deep breath, holding it in for a couple seconds, and forcefully exhaling. Have you heard of Lamaze style breathing? Lamaze classes were all the rage when my mother was having children. The "Hee-hee-hoo" breathing technique is a conscious breathing technique that focuses on slow, deep breaths. It was originally referred to as the psychoprophylactic method. Translated from Greek, it is an advanced, mental guard to overcome pain. Conscious breathing can help a person relax and feel in control during labor. Gaining control, in the moment, of my thoughts and focus took unprecedented importance in the battlefield of my mind. As I slowed my breathing, I began reciting the truth from Philippians 4:7. My army's commanding officer offers His peace that transcends all understanding to guard my heart and *my* mind in Christ Jesus.

How do we hold ground towards victory?

If breathing helped regain control of my battlefield, I needed a way to hold fast until victory. The answer came directly from the verse which precedes the Philippians verse mentioned above about peace that surpasses all understanding:

"Do not be anxious about anything, but in everything, by prayer and petition, with thanksgiving, present your requests to God."
Philippians 4:6

Battle anxiety with thankfulness. It can't be that simple, right? In his book What Happy People Know, Dan Baker states, "It is a fact of neurology that the brain cannot be in a state of appreciation and a state of fear at the same time. The two states may alternate, but are mutually exclusive" (Baker, 81).[17] When my focus turns from anxious what if, fearful spirals, to thank the Lord for what He has done, I physically feel the shift in my mental state. Start small, thank Him for the sun that reminds us of His renewed love for us every morning, the ability to wake up that day, or the privilege of freewill. As you start thanking Him for the things that we take for granted, you can start thanking Him for His promises of a sound mind, His peace that surpasses our understanding, and health for our whole bodies. Those things may not be physically experienced, but His words don't come back void.

We can thank our trustworthy, heavenly Father for designing our brains to reboot from anxiety attacks by focusing on thankfulness.

➡ **Jump to pages 76-80 in the Full Hands, Full Life Activity Companion Guide for this week's interactive prompts.**

Full Hands, Full Life

Week 14: Self-Image

If we're honest, there are things about our physical appearance we just don't like. If this wasn't true, then cosmetic plastic surgeons, cosmetologists, and the beauty industry would go out of business. Perhaps your list contains your eye color, hair texture, freckles, weight, scars, stretch marks, body size, or proportions.

A big one for me growing up was my smile. My front two teeth crossed like an X; I could fit my pinky under my overbite, and the bottom row alignment gained inspiration from the chevron pattern. Unfortunately there's no quick, easy fix for an adolescent girl who wants a new smile. My smile became a weak spot for me. I remember one set of family portraits where my mom, dad, older sister, and I all matched in fancy, paper white outfits for an outdoor photo shoot. While getting dressed, my mom made a comment about how she wanted me "to smile a genuine smile like my older sister" during the pictures. My sister, to this day, has perfect teeth. Her teeth are so straight you assume she came out of the womb wearing braces. She could smile all day long with all her pearly whites showing, but she had this gentle lips-together smile that made her blue eyes twinkle.

Her perfect teeth didn't even show! The act of smiling forced my teeth to show because as I curled the corners of my lips up my crossed, overbite ridden buck teeth forced my lips apart! I stood in front of the mirror and tried to master this gentle, lip closed smile for several minutes before it was picture time.

My smile was anything but genuine that day. I successfully kept my lips together, hiding what I instantly decided was an unsightly flaw to my family. The framed canvas picture of that moment still hangs on my parent's wall today. My expression reminds me of the old-timey photos where the kids had to be motionless and almost lifeless for ten minutes or the picture would turn out blurry. My self-consciousness about my smile came to an all-time high that day. Getting braces on couldn't come soon enough.

For some families, the financial burden for braces can be a non-starter. Thankfully, my parents footed the bill, making braces an option for me, but I had to wait for the magic number of adult teeth to be in place for the journey to begin. Once I got the green light for braces, the estimated two year process ended up being a four year overhaul. The day I got my brackets removed made all the bands and pain and flossing worth it—I felt confident in my new smile. The orthodontist made a mold of my teeth for retainers. Seven short days later, I went back for the retainer, and the dental assistant barely got it in my mouth. The pain was real. My orthodontist was shocked at how quickly my teeth had shifted but assured me if I wore my retainers around the clock, the nerves would catch up in my mouth to hold the teeth in place.

Off I went with my royal purple wire retainers. About a month or so in, I left my retainer on the lunch tray at school. I mustered up the courage to come clean about it to my parents when they asked why I didn't have my retainer in after school. That's when I found out that new retainers cost $400 and I must be more responsible. By the time my appointment came up, I had to have another mold made because my teeth shifted so quickly that the original mold would not suffice. Another week later, I was on the way home, with achy teeth and a new glittery, green retainer.

Twelve months later, when I graduated from the orthodontist and was approved for night-only wear of the retainer, my Jack Russell terrier, Duplin, snuck my retainer from the bathroom sink and destroyed it. Now, this was a big conundrum for my teenage self. Duplin was already on a thin leash with my folks. We lived on a small, six-acre horse farm, and had dozens of animals, but Duplin was a bit unpredictable. She was a rescue and far less trained than our other animals. Her uncharacteristically long legs for the Jack Russell breed made her tall enough to sneak things off the counter, and when she got these prized possessions, her aggressive guarding nature took over. I just knew if I mentioned the retainer was her fault, she was a goner. So months, then years passed, and my teeth shifted and shifted. They never returned fully to their original disarray, but they certainly crossed significantly in the front again and the bottom row overcrowded.

Fast forward seven years, at the young age of twenty-two, the love of my life proposed to me. Just a couple months later the wedding arrangements were made, and bridal portrait day arrived. We treated my bridal portraits as a test drive for all wedding day beauty routines. My hair stylist perfected the low bun of loose curls framing my neck, my makeup accentuated all the right features, and with the last set of dress alterations complete, my dress fit like a glove. As I was exiting the dressing room in a historic downtown home rented out for the bridal portraits, I glanced in the mirror one last time and beamed with excitement. I turned to my mom and said, "Thank you. I truly feel like a princess." To that she said I did look stunning and followed it up with, "...and, maybe after the wedding you can work on getting your teeth fixed again." I mean, talk about a self-conscious attack! Knock me down a notch! It was a high to a low, ladies—a real high to a real mental low. Bless my mom's loving heart. I'm sure she never would have let those words come out of her mouth if she knew how much it stung. She voiced the only thing I was feeling self conscious about as I looked in the mirror, and my teeth were about to be on full display. I couldn't get the comment out of my mind for the picture session and although I love my bridal portraits, I look at the pictures and reflect on the day, I don't remember any of the other conversations with the clarity of those exchanges. I'm sure my mom was thinking practically about how entering this exciting new phase in life as a married adult would make the choice to work on my teeth again a reality. But, we hadn't even talked about whether I disliked my teeth.

A year into marriage, I got Invisalign. My husband, Chris, mentioned he loved how my teeth crossed in the front just a bit and might be sad to see it go. Imagine that, the one thing I was so self conscious about was something that my husband found endearing and beautiful.

Now, two decades later I could probably stand to have another round of Invisalign because my teeth have shifted yet again, but I've learned some strong truths about the God of the universe who created me. When insecurities and self conscious thoughts creep in, I have found such solace in two discoveries in the Bible:

1. We are made in God's very image.
2. We are fearfully and wonderfully made.

In the beginning, yes, even before the creation of Adam and Eve, God said, "Let us make man in our image, in our likeness..." (Genesis 1:26). The honor of being created in God's image was saved for His last creation: humans. We are the only beings on this Earth that get to bear His own image and likeness. This is a blessing and a gift.

Psalm 139:14 offers a beautiful declaration to say over yourself when self-consciousness rears its ugly head: "I praise you because I am fearfully and wonderfully made; your works are wonderful, I know that full well." The Lord created you, not with reckless abandon, not with ordinary and common blueprints. He made you fearfully—cautiously, with a devised plan, and wonderfully—delightfully, superbly, set apart from the rest.

Sometimes the faults others point out about our bodies can make those features scream loudest when we face a mirror. As a mother, these comments still circle around in my mind. I desperately want to avoid creating lifelong insecurities in my own children. For instance, when one of my young girls show up by the back door for a special outing in an outfit that arguably doesn't match, there is a big difference between saying, "Great job getting dressed, but real quick let's try to find solid color pants that match one color in that fun top, or a solid color top that matches a color in those favorite flower pants!" Instead of "Wow, I can't believe you chose that outfit. You have no fashion sense. I'll still be having to dress you when you go to college."

Just yesterday I was getting in the car on our way to church and found my five year old with the most stained white sweatshirt she owned and fruit print pants. I was shocked and said, "Hmmm, that doesn't seem like your normal choice for church. Did you pick that because you got paint on your dress last week at church?" To which she answered, "Yes. I think we will be painting again and I want to be ready." On some mornings I would have just let it slide, but this particular Sunday, they were singing for the entire congregation. I quickly said, "Good thinking, but you are singing in 'big church' today so I don't think you will have time for painting. I'll run in real quick and get the outfit you told me yesterday you were excited to wear this morning." She kept her confidence about not only her decision-making in thinking through wearing something already stained, just in case, but also her confidence in being able to make choices on outfits that matched because I brought out another outfit she put together. It was a win-win, but they haven't always turned out that way.

When I give my kids criticisms about an outfit or a physical attribute, I carefully try to craft the words in a loving way which praises their willingness to try and gently guide them towards the goal I believe they had in mind in the first place. With five daughters, dress up clothes abound in our home. When the littles play dress up and parade around, my husband always makes a point to say how "fancy" they look instead of how "beautiful" they look, and we add in comments about how the dresses, high heels, and make-up don't make them beautiful. True beauty is from the inside out, not the outside in.

Words can change the genuineness of our smiles in the short run, or if left unchecked, can change the trajectory of our mental state and cause us to lose motivation towards accomplishing lifelong goals. Many times comments from others stem from their own insecurities. Sometimes they are warranted. Sometimes they are just meant to hurt. Regardless, words can't be taken back and what we do with criticism holds major weight on our future. Meditating daily on the truth that the Lord delights in the way He meticulously created you, and loves you the way you are right now with all your shiny attributes and even the blemishes, can bring about feelings of wholeness. And, who knows. Maybe He even created someone out there who finds what you see as your biggest physical flaw endearing like He did for me. The inscription I had engraved inside my husband's wedding ring reads, "God made you with me in mind." Little did I know in making Chris, the God of the universe cared about me so deeply that he took time to form the smallest of details including him finding cuteness in my curtseying front teeth.

➡️ **Jump to pages 82-86 in the Full Hands, Full Life Activity Companion Guide for this week's interactive prompts.**

Week 15: Personal Sacrifice

When asked about the most selfless act you could do for another person, aside from giving your life for them, bearing a child tops the list. By choosing to give your child life, you are allowing life to be sustained from your own life itself. Without your daily sacrifice, the child would have no chance for survival.

Honor exists in sacrifice. Bravery exists in sacrifice, but in worldly standards, loss is equated with sacrifice. Perhaps becoming pregnant meant losing a job, money, or housing, or a dream put on hold. Regardless of the tangible worldly losses pregnancy potentially brings on, there is one fundamental sacrifice that is made—your body. That particular sacrifice brought on the most anxiety for me each pregnancy.

Eating disorders plagued my years in high school and college. At my lowest point, I only ate a couple hundred calories a day. I threw my food out the window on the way to school justifying that I was feeding the birds (taking off the wrapper first, of course . . . I didn't want to litter!). Then I skipped lunch and explained to my friends that I was going to eat right after school. They believed me because I got out of school early to go teach piano keyboard classes at an underprivileged Title I elementary school across town. Then I worked at a local seafood house at night. If you have ever worked in a restaurant, you know it can be a double-edged sword. At first, the easy access to food can be such a blessing, but after a while you can't imagine eating that food anymore. So, my dinner would be two packets of saltine crackers with cocktail sauce.

I thought my anorexia was going undetected until one day during school. As a high school senior, I got the opportunity to help my choir director with our school's varsity choir, "Capital Pride." Being an accomplished pianist at the time, I often took a section of the choir into the large costume closet with an upright piano to work on parts. Since the boys' sections typically had fewer members, frequently I would have a section of the guys. Many of these guys were some of my best friends. On one occasion I remember one of these guys, who knew me on a deeper level than the rest, pulling me aside and saying, "I'm not sure what's going on, but you are disappearing. I'm worried and want you to know that it doesn't seem good." Sadly, my mind was so twisted at the time that I saw this as the ultimate compliment instead of a warning sign. What it did do was confirm the eyes I was using to look in the mirror were lying to me. I saw no difference. The scale was trending down, clothes were no longer fitting, but I saw major room for improvement. I sought control of something in my life since so many other things were spiraling out of control. I'm thankful for him being willing to step in and say what others were unwilling to say. It was a stake in the ground for recognizing the problem, but I wasn't in the head space yet to allow it to be the turning point.

Once in college, the open buffets and dining hall experiences with friends became a problem for me. I wasn't familiar with the sensation of a full stomach. I would eat and eat, which is what everyone else seemed to be doing, but then felt sick. My anorexia turned to bulimia. I purged after I ate. I even knew how much water needed to be drunk in order to make it easier. I worked out every day of the week. If I couldn't work out, then I punished myself by not eating. Self image insecurities surfaced in the seclusion of my dorm room. Without a roommate, my battle with eating disorders grew to an all time high.

By the first semester of my junior year, I finally realized I couldn't keep up this lifestyle. I sought counseling from the university health department. Within just a few sessions, I quickly discovered the why behind my eating disorders—striving to please people and realize perfection that life can't provide. I sought after control in caloric intake and body image. See, our hearts are created with a Jesus-shaped hole no worldly success or attention from people can fill. At any point during my struggle, if someone had spoken truths to me about my beauty and worth in my Heavenly Father's eyes and the price He had already paid for me by sending His only son, Jesus, to die on the cross for me and my shortcomings, my years of body image struggles could have come to an end. I wouldn't have ended up twenty-five pounds underweight and seeking approval from all the wrong people in all the wrong places. That truth didn't sink in for a couple more years even as I continued to pursue professional help.

My counselor shared practical how-to's I could put into practice. Our sessions were right before Thanksgiving. I was anxious about letting down members of my extended family when I didn't try heaping portions of their beloved recipes. She suggested I either use a dinner plate and not go back for seconds or use a smaller salad plate and go back for any foods I couldn't fit on my plate the first time around. What a perfectly normal and easy strategy! I changed my need for control into a healthier solution—portion sizes—and made breakthroughs in healthy eating strategies. My energy soared. My concentration came back.

You can imagine how getting pregnant less than two years after these breakthroughs in freedom from eating disorders brought on a wave of anxiety. The battles I thought I fought and won plagued my mind again because I hadn't treated the root of the problem. I didn't want to compromise the safety and growth of my son by my unwillingness to let my body grow along with him. While pregnant, I worked out every day and cared deeply about the nutrition I was taking in. I decided if I was going to be eating for two, it better be the healthiest food out there. I specifically remember going to Chick-fil-A with my husband and deciding to eat french fries just one time during that pregnancy and feeling guilty. But, allowing my body to grow and give my son life ultimately changed my own life. I realized my sacrifice allowed the Lord to create a new image bearer of Himself that I got to witness from the inside out. My son changed my perception of body image and the love our heavenly Father has for us. If I loved my son an indescribable amount and that was only a shadow of the love God has for me, then I no longer needed to seek after love from this world in imperfect people. I was looking for something I already had waiting for me to accept from Him.

If you are in the midst of pregnancy and struggle with eating disorders, or feel discouraged by your post-pregnancy shape, please know you are not alone. My prayer is you start focusing on the positive side of allowing your body to change. You opened the door for your child to walk into this life alongside you. 2 Chronicles 15:7 states, "But as for you, be brave and don't lose heart, because your work will be rewarded!" Your body grew a reward in your child. Take it day by day. Remember the sacrificial role you played in your child's life is an honorable one that the Lord hand chose you to play. So make healthy choices for you and your baby's body and put on those maternity clothes (or the next size up) with a sense of honor and pride. Your beauty radiates from the inside out.

➡️ **Jump to pages 88-92 in the Full Hands, Full Life Activity Companion Guide for this week's interactive prompts.**

Week 16: Disappointment / Curveballs of Life

On the scale of "you have a 4-page birth plan printed, laminated, and already in your hospital bag," to "you hope your nurse gives good advice," which are you or were you heading into delivery? For our first, I had a scheduled C-section. My plan went completely out the window at 36 weeks when he was a frank breech. If you're not familiar with that position, the baby is basically sitting in your belly like a Buddha statue. On ultrasounds, Brooks actually sucked on his toes. For a solid twenty-four hours after he was born, every time we would pull his legs down his feet would perfectly fly back up to his neck. My mom always said, "C-section babies are just the prettiest," and she was right. He was precious. His face was absolutely perfect—no smooshed baby look or cone head, just a perfect Little Magoo—but it wasn't what I intended.

Leading up to my first delivery, I had all the time in the world to read books, watch documentaries, and Google birth plans; however, with Brooks being my first, his compromised position, my low fluid levels, and an anterior placenta, doctors manually trying to move him into a "birthable position" was too risky to attempt. From all those factors, plus the handstands in the pool and countless inversion stair laying sessions to promote him naturally flipping, I felt justified that I was not "giving up" by having a C-section. Plus, no indications existed that future v-BACs were out of the question for me.

Eight months into our second pregnancy, I dusted off all the birth plan materials. I researched the latest and greatest new findings in birthing and was ready to go. Baby was head down; things were looking great. One night I had so many contractions I felt certain I was going into labor, but Chris was out of town. I printed my birth plan and waited to call him to fly home, but the contractions stopped. I held out until my 42 week checkup (yes, two full weeks past my due date) to hear that Ellie's heart rate was drastically low, and we needed an emergency C-section. I was so sure I was getting induced the next day as scheduled, I hadn't even brought my hospital bag to the appointment!

During the non-stress test appointment, the doctor insisted I drink a Mountain Dew to try to get her heart rate up. Perhaps she was just experiencing low sugar. Well, I never drank caffeine, so that was a shock to me and sweet baby Ellie. About the time the caffeine was in full swing, my C-section was ending, and Ellie's blood sugar levels were all out of whack. They rushed her off to the nursery for monitoring, pricking her heels every ten minutes, while refusing to bring her to me because of arrhythmias on my heart monitor. Imagine that—a woman who was pumped full of caffeine, whose all-natural birth plan was thrown out the window, and whose baby was being kept completely out of sight was having irregular heartbeats. What should have been obviously explained by the circumstances was being exacerbated by the doctor's unwillingness to discuss the problem with me. They feared telling me why she was being kept away as they didn't want to make the heart problems worse.

The heart monitor arrhythmias increased in frequency during this caffeine and hormonally induced state, which helped me muster up the courage to demand my baby and husband be returned to my bedside. Once I had her nursing in my arms, my heartbeat normalized, her blood sugar levels regulated, and we were on our recovery path together, but the trauma had already ensued.

I felt like a failure and the thoughts which followed confirmed that. How could the Lord make my body able to grow babies but not birth babies? What was wrong with me? Would I ever get to experience the natural birth I wanted and really felt strong enough to endure? Would this second C-section mean I couldn't have any other children VBAC?

Long story short, having our third just sixteen months later made C-sections the only option for all the rest!

For years, I wrestled with the disappointment and feelings of failure from having to have C-sections. I felt like a less-than mother. Like it wasn't as real. Since this is an emotional safe space between us, I'll share that I even felt relieved when others had to have them too. I wasn't alone in my body refusing to allow natural births. Knowing I was wrestling with these thoughts, my sweet husband would remind me that if we lived hundreds of years ago, both Brooks and I would likely have not survived childbirth. He would talk about how convenient they were (aside from the recovery part, of course). So the shame was all self-inflicted. I didn't know if I would ever gain a healthy perspective on delivering my children via C-section.

Life throws us curveballs. How we react to them is based on what our foundation lies on. The Apostle Paul knew all about the disappointments and curveballs in life. He was flogged five times with the Jews' thirty-nine lashes (one lashing short of death), beaten by Roman rods three times, pummeled with rocks once, shipwrecked three times, and immersed in the open sea for a night and a day. Yet, this same man wrote these words in his letter to the Romans:

"We also have joy with our troubles, because we know that these troubles produce patience. And patience produces character, and character produces hope. And this hope will never disappoint us, because God has

> *poured out his love to fill our hearts."*
> Romans 5:3-5 (New Century Version)

Find joy in our troubles? It can't be that easy, can it? During week 13, we learned thankfulness and fear cannot coexist in the mind. Perhaps a similar correlation exists between joy and suffering.

Realizing this unhealthy mental attitude towards my deliveries, I started focusing on the truths of the matter, the things out of my control. My body showed clear signs that I could not safely deliver babies any other way. I found joy that we are living in a time where this surgery is a safer option than in centuries past. I found patience in waiting for my uterus to grow strong enough before having more children each time. I found character through enjoying the stages of life with each of my healthy, growing children. I found hope in helping friends grieving their shattered birth plans realize their birth plan ended up exactly how it needed to be to increase the likelihood of a safe delivery for them and their baby.

Through my six experiences, I get to encourage moms that they will feel the sensation of delivery as a weightlessness comes over your spine when they lift that squinty-eyed, wiggly baby from your stomach, and you hear their first cry. I also have a unique perspective on the twelve-year progression I witnessed in healthcare's focus to keep the mom and baby together post operation. I had tears streaming down my cheeks when they asked if I wanted skin-on-skin bonding time immediately after birth while still on the operating table with my fourth. I get to share how I held my fifth in my arms as we were wheeled to our recovery room together. By my sixth, I was able to witness the footprints and hair washing the first time ever because she never left my sight. I get to pass on what I hope to be my top four tips for friends expecting C-sections:

1. If you have a tall bed, take the matress off the bed frame to make getting in and out of bed easier.

2. If your room is upstairs, plan on having everything you need up there for a few days—and be OK with it! Enjoy the fewer distractions and extra baby snuggles.
3. For the first 48-72 hours, keep a small pillow or book nearby to press against your incision area if you need to cough, sneeze, or laugh. I promise it helps!
4. Use gallon size bags to make meals ahead of time and freeze them with instructions written on the outside, so a few meals can be made with no questions asked.

Now, I can listen to birth stories in wonder, while marveling at how unique and beautiful they all are. The joy I've had in sharing my stories with women throughout the past decade and a half brings me hope that I can find joy in all my troubles.

If you are currently in a season of disappointment or feel life has thrown you a curveball, my prayer is that you will find joy in the trouble. May patience, character, and hope find you quickly. If the Apostle Paul could endure his level of suffering and still experience a joy that never disappoints, I have confidence the Heavenly Father we all share in common still pours the same love out for us.

**➡ Jump to pages 94-98 in the
Full Hands, Full Life Activity Companion Guide
for this week's interactive prompts.**

Full Hands, Full Life

Week 17: Strongholds of Addiction

When I turned thirty-nine, I found coffee. I know. The discovery wasn't revolutionary for the world at large, but for me, it was a newfangled luxury. Until that point, I was never the girl wearing the "Living on Jesus & Coffee" t-shirt (which I think are so darn cute, mind you. I just felt like a hypocrite purchasing one because I never drank coffee). People would want to set up meetings over coffee, and I'd ask if the place had smoothies. I went to so many coffee shops over the years envying my friends who had "their" drink order perfected for each café in town. I also never drank caffeine. I grew up in a caffeine-free home, so it never became a crux. Fresca was the special treat in our pantry, but we either had to plan ahead or put it over ice because it never held a permanent spot in the fridge.

Something about turning my last year before forty got in my head. I found a new pep in my step when I drank coffee one day, then I decided to have another coffee the next day. Before I knew it, I had my pecan praline coffee with dairy free caramel macchiato creamer made to perfection every morning. Why had I been depriving myself of such a treat of extra energy given my six kids and various jobs and responsibilities over the years? I was in utter shock. All the t-shirts and slogans made sense. I found myself excited to get up to spend time with Jesus because I would have my warm coffee alongside my Bible.

But just as quickly as the coffee craze entered my life at thirty-nine, it fled when I turned forty. I started having convictions about how my mood instantly changed when I was in the middle of homeschooling one of the kids and realized I had more coffee left. It was an instant boost. My cup in the morning started becoming the first of the day followed by another one at about 2 o'clock—because why not? Right?! I started realizing I was on a slippery slope. Yes, we are still talking about coffee, but a crux is a crux for me. Instead of coffee bringing my mood up, I found my mood was down unless coffee was included with the kids. I was lacking patience when I knew my patience could not have already been depleted in a day; after all, it wasn't even 9am! I started wondering if I would still get up early if the coffee wasn't part of my morning routine. Would I be as excited to jump start my morning with Jesus alone?

As these thoughts were swirling through my head, I decided to skip coffee one day. The headache was out of this world. Nothing touched it. It was a short-lived attempt at giving up coffee. It was so short lived, I had my 2pm coffee to curb the throbbing in my head. My kids knew something was up and offered to make the coffee themselves. My heart was fully convicted, but reluctant to acknowledge the reality of the situation. For a week, I tried to convince myself that my conviction was about the amount of sugar I was drinking from the creamer. So, I used less creamer, but the coffee tasted horrible. I tried different creamers. I tried different brands of coffee. I even tried using less water in the coffee so that I didn't have to use as much creamer altogether. Nothing made the nagging feeling go away that it just wasn't worth it. Something wasn't right.

One Sunday morning, I was serving as part of the worship team at church. A friend from our church community group that meets on Wednesday nights was serving on the worship team that weekend as well. As she ate what looked like a delicious morning hash, we chatted about the clean eating plan she was on that was making her feel amazing. She shared the first two days were tragic and she felt awful, but it had been helping her create healthy habits that made her feel so much better every day since. I felt a twinge in my heart again from the Holy Spirit to lean in and listen. During our break between services, I told her I was going to start the clean eating program the very next day, and I would check in with her on my progress. She became my accountability partner in the whole fiasco and knew my main goal was to also cut out the coffee. As I saw it, I was going to feel as horrible giving up caffeine from coffee as I did about giving up the sugar, gluten, and dairy, so why not do it all at once and know I was making clean choices along the way? Sounds brutal, but I've never been one to shy away from diving all in on something others found impossible.

After just three days, the most amazing thing happened. I started seeing my patience return. I started regaining control over my emotions. I started gaining a preview of the responses I nearly spat out at my kids and the angry mom glare spread across my eyes, so I could make a different choice. The caffeine I was so eager to make excuses to add in actually depleted me of the necessary resources to be the mom the Lord created me to be.

Now, I'm not trying to make a case for everyone to give up coffee or even caffeine. I'm just sharing how what I thought helped me throughout the day was actually making my days tougher to get through. I tangibly felt the Holy Spirit convicting my heart, and the further I tried to run from it or make a secondary path around the issue, the harder the Spirit pushed me towards quitting cold turkey.

The temptation to make a coffee is in front of me every day. After a couple weeks, I threw away the creamer taking up residence in the fridge. I put the coffee maker back in the laundry room cabinet (where it lived unless we had company staying over because what kind of hostess would I be if I couldn't make a person a cup of Joe for breakfast?). But the coffee grounds are still on the counter. The cute basket my girls made me for all my coffee paraphernalia is next to the toaster. It would be really easy to make an undetected cup of coffee. But I would still know.

1 Corinthians 10:13 has brought me great confidence over the past several months. "No temptation has overtaken you except what is common to mankind. And God is faithful; He will not let you be tempted beyond what you can bear. But when you are tempted, He will also provide a way out so that you can endure it." I can stand up under the weight of temptations as long as I continue looking for the way out the Lord promises to provide. You can stand up with this same confidence as well.

Are there things in your daily life you feel you could label as cruxes? Things you wrap your self-worth in being able to keep going? Actions you take that make you happy, even if they aren't in your best interest? Although addictions typically get siloed into alcohol, substance abuse, or drug use, they can take on many different forms like shopping, food consumption, and even video gaming. If nothing comes to mind for you personally, you likely have someone within your sphere of influence who daily battles a form of addiction.

The good news is there is no crux too deep, grave, or habitual that God cannot forgive. He wants to walk with us to freedom. John 8:35-36 says "Now a slave has no permanent place in the family, but a son belongs to it forever. So if the Son sets you free, you will be free indeed." Jesus has called us all into His family as daughters of the Most High King. Of that we can be sure. And since we have been set free from our past sins, we now only have to look for the way out which the Lord provides, and have the strength and conviction to walk through it.

For me, the conviction behind the coffee crux had a two day turnaround time. Sure I could relapse because no one would bat an eye at a mother drinking a cup of

Battling Mindsets

coffee. Only I would feel the conviction. For others of us, the addiction may be easier to pinpoint and much harder to avoid. Perhaps it will take weeks, even months to find victory. Whatever is stirring in your heart as you read these words, whether it is something specifically in your life or in the life of someone around you, ask the Lord to show you the next right step. Having an accountability partner along the way helped immensely. I highly recommend finding someone who is strong in the area that you are weak to be a trusted accountability partner. As the Lord sent my friend on the worship team to me, He will help you find your next step as well. Just be willing to step into the way out He provides. If it is giving guidance in the life of others, go to the Lord in prayer for that person. When a safe opportunity arises, perhaps in the company of others, and in love, open up the conversation on the subject. May you find freedom from everything that may be hindering you from being the mother you want to be and creating the environment you want for raising your children.

➡ **Jump to pages 100-104 in the Full Hands, Full Life Activity Companion Guide for this week's interactive prompts.**

Full Hands, Full Life

Week 18: Fear

When I was in my third trimester of my second pregnancy, my motherhood bubble shattered. On vacation, my husband and I left our son, not even two at the time, at the beach house with our family to grab a bite of ice cream. Since it was nearing bedtime for Brooks, we felt confident our decision to leave him was the best choice. We planned on having this mini-date at the local, homemade ice cream shop and erase all evidence of the outing taking place before we came back home. As a first-time mom, I always erred on the side of caution, and some may say I was borderline overprotective. There was a time period when I would not allow anyone to drive Brooks around. Leaving him at the beach house was a feat in and of itself.

About halfway through our ice cream scoops, we got the dreaded call, "Brooks fell face-first onto the leg of the table. He split his upper lip wide open. He is going to be okay, but he wants his mommy pretty bad." Y'all, I wasn't there for the fall and even worse, wasn't there to comfort him through the pain. We could not get back fast enough. His lip, already swollen twice its size, was protruding from his sweet little mouth. The laceration went halfway up to his nose. I couldn't keep from thinking about how this sweet little baby would have a spot in his mustache that would never grow hair. He'd have a scar on his upper lip and I couldn't even describe the event that caused it because I had left him and wasn't a witness. We consulted my father-in-law, who happens to not only be an incredibly humble, loving, Christ-following grandfather, but conveniently an impeccable ENT and reconstructive facial plastic surgeon. Ultimately, based on Brooks' age, how quickly the mouth heals, and the proximity of the laceration to the mouth, we opted to use the paci as a band-aid to hold the wound together instead of putting him through the trauma of stitches.

I'll never forget the conversation between Chris and me that night as we retreated to our bedroom with Brooks to process the event together. Being eight months pregnant, I felt our baby girl moving in my belly while my twenty-three month old lay hurting in my arms. Chris encouraged me to stop playing the "if only" game outlining the mirage of scenarios that ended with Brooks not being injured. He reminded me of all the good choices we make daily as parents. He reminded me of the original reason we had left him at the house with our loving, trustworthy family who had watched him incident-free countless times before. He reminded me it was a freak accident, and accidents are called that for a reason, but we both felt a wave of nausea in the pit of our stomachs. I turned to Chris with tear-filled eyes and said, "I can't even keep one safe. I don't think I'm cut out to be trusted with another and the next one will be here in just a few weeks!"

Over a decade and five more children later, I can say that living through fearful situations does make us stronger. The same son I was torn up about having a little scar above his lip was helping me trim hedges in our backyard a year ago. As he trimmed down the side of a severely overgrown bush, gravity got the best of the hedge trimmers, and they grazed his left thigh making a deep, zig zag pattern. When I asked if he wanted to get it stitched, he said, "Nah, it will make a great story one day." Bless him.

Going into motherhood with a general fear of the unknown is honestly a good sign you are on your way to being a great parent. Channeling that fear into protection and smart decision-making as a parent is a healthy avenue. However, if fear is left unchecked, it could become crippling to your ability to enjoy the ebbs and flows of motherhood. In extreme cases, it can also lead to stifling a child's growth towards adulthood.

In his letter to Timothy, Paul encourages his child in the faith with this truth, "For God has not given us a spirit of fear, but of power and of love and of a sound mind" (2 Timothy 1:7 New King James Version). Speak these words over and over in your mind. It is a TRUTH you can stand on. The Lord's Word does not come back void. As mothers, we can ask God for deliverance from a spirit of fear. If you are currently pregnant and fearing delivery, be honest with the Lord and tell Him. If you have a C-section date scheduled and fear the surgery and recovery with an infant in tow, share that burden with the Lord. If you're nursing and you fear there isn't enough milk to satisfy your baby, ask the Lord for guidance. If you have a baby turning into a toddler who seems to tumble and fall more than your heart can take the adrenaline roller coaster, ask Him to enter into those times of fear and protect your child when you can't.

As mothers, our children need us to stay attuned to the perils of this world. When babies, they need us to follow safety protocols. As they grow, we must make smart choices in public spaces like keeping them in eyesight in grocery stores and staying attentive at local parks, but we also must allow the safeguards we put in place to grow proportionately with them. Our goal as mothers is not to raise adult-sized babies, but to grow independent, contributing members of society. My prayer is that as our children (mine and yours) move into adulthood, they would deeply know the love of Jesus and use Him as their guiding light, contrary to where the worldly standards may be pulling them.

Ultimately, whether we currently feel it or not, we can thank the Lord for giving us the spirit of power, love, and a sound mind in our role as mothers. We can ask Him to turn our spirit of fear into a spirit of wisdom and discernment. The overprotective mother I was to my first little baby is only a shadow of the mother I am today, but she is part of my journey. For now, I encourage you to simply look introspectively for places where fear may be stealing some of your joy in motherhood and start praying for the spirit of fear to be replaced with a spirit of power, love, and a sound mind.

➡️ **Jump to pages 106-110 in the Full Hands, Full Life Activity Companion Guide for this week's interactive prompts.**

Week 19: Perfection Not Needed

The *gold standard* determines the value of a country's currency in relation to a set weight of gold. How? By the rigorous adherents to *the standard* remaining fixed to compare currencies from different countries. Do you know how gold is purified to meet *the standard*? This precious metal does not exist in pure form. Gold must be melted so the impurities that rise to the top can be skimmed off. I don't know about you, but I don't want to be an impurity floating around in gold–an imposter. I want to be refined gold, priced at full value, impurity free.

However, perfection is something none of us are capable of achieving. Wow, my heart needed to hear that so let's say it again. None of us are capable of achieving perfection. It's impossible, so take that burden off your shoulders.

To me, motherhood is a long purification process. Sometimes my impurities surface as I watch my mini-me's respond to one another as if I said things myself, sass and all! Sometimes they surface from decisions I make which backfire (like deciding at the last minute to curl my hair before leaving, which causes us to all be running to the car with breakfast and shoes in hand). Sometimes it shows up in bigger ways that incite a parenting reboot.

Our older daughters take dance classes at a high level, Christian fine arts academy in our hometown. With so many littles, I opt to not spend hours in the lobby entertaining my youngest daughters while the older ones are in class, so I trust my children to exercise self-control, be respectful, and behave well during breaks. Unfortunately, when left unchecked, this level of personal responsibility can prove too much for an eight-year-old with an hour long dinner break. Natalie, our bubbly, creative thinker with a contagious laugh, loved dinner hour. She begged weekly to get to stay and hang out with her friends as her older sisters finished up their classes for the evening. Since we homeschool, her time with friends is important to her growth, so I value this opportunity as well.

One evening, Natalie and her friends made their way into the bathroom to wash sticky hands. Great decision. Who wants sticky hands touching seats, tables, carpets, and dance attire? But this bathroom happened to be the furthest away from the lobby. Some might argue it was out of ear shot entirely. This particular bathroom also had a faucet with the water pressure of a fire hose. An unsuspecting handwasher could receive a shocking frontside spritz, and that night, the spritz turned into a full-blown splash pad! Typically one would quickly shut off the valve and readjust, but Natalie and her friends could not gather their wits beyond the tears of laughter.

With the water billowing over the sides of the sink and puddles forming on the linoleum floor, one of the littles managed to wade their way over to turn off the faucet. Then reality hit. They made a huge mess. In our home, we grab towels and make a game of skating around to clean up messes. At the studio, the commercial school paper towels are better at moving liquids around than actually absorbing them. So, paper towel after paper towel was thrown on the puddles. Little feet were skating to the best of their ability to dry the floor. Dinner hour was over and moms started calling their littles. Being good listeners, they obeyed their mothers and left one by one. Everyone, including Natalie, assumed the friends who were left would finish the job. The last one frantically left as his mom's voice called his name a second time and the bathroom looked like it had been rolled in paper towels with a water hose left running.

Unaware of the situation, the moms—myself included—took our littles home for the night. The office manager, Mrs. Chrissy, who closed up for the night, has an admirable gift for gracefully speaking into uncomfortable conversations with love and authority, and sent our mom group a heartfelt text message after closing. Natalie and I discussed the situation and set up a consequence of losing her coveted hangout during dinner time with friends for two weeks. I felt like I won the mom's response game. I made sure she was taking this seriously to avoid similar situations in the future. I expressed the importance of communicating with us moms if there is a mess that warrants extra clean up time before leaving. We would all understand that! I also explained that we can't take advantage of the kindness and inclusion they allow at the dance studio. I thanked her for being honest with me and being willing to talk about the situation with me. Even though she vehemently explained she was not one of the ones that lined the floor with paper towels or used the toilet brush as a floor swiffer, it gave us an opportunity to talk about the notion of "guilty by association."

The next evening, I spoke with one of the other moms from the text thread about how she handled the situation. Her response blew my mind. She not only talked with her children about it, established a consequence where they would sit with her for the next two weeks while playing within a ten foot radius from her so she could better hear and see what was going on, but as part of the "righting the wrong," she had them also each go individually and apologize in person to Mrs. Chrissy! What an obvious apples to apples response that offered closure for their maturing hearts. She explained that what you did in secret you must voice out loud and give the person who you wronged the opportunity to accept the apology. But more importantly, you must show you understand that what you did was wrong and you are sorry for making the mistake.

The next day Natalie had dance class, I had her go and apologize to Mrs. Chrissy in person—looking her in the eyes. It is not out of shame that we apologize; it is out of the desire to help foster relationships and move beyond the incident to a deeper space.

For many of us, someone with a humble, contrite spirit wasn't exemplified within our own homes. Apologies can be hard because they require admitting a wrong, which many aren't willing to do. In that case, we are left to learn how to apologize on our own. I would venture to say I was well into my thirties before my inability to apologize the "right" way was brought to my attention. Many times after apologizing, I found the person I apologized to turning around and apologizing to me. How could my mistake now have the other person showing remorse for the situation? Healthy apologies are never followed up with a "but." For instance, "I'm sorry what I said made you feel that way, but you were not being helpful and you needed to be called out." A genuine apology sounds like, "I'm so sorry I let my frustration come out at you. I shouldn't have said or done that and won't do it again." That's progress.

We are all responsible for our own bodies, including the words we speak and the actions of our hands and feet. Jesus wants us to be so deeply rooted in His love and peace that nobody's actions can cause us to stumble and lash out verbally or physically.

As a mom, this can be tough. Nothing can make me feel more out of control and immature than lashing out at my two-year old for doing a very age appropriate thing. A week after her second birthday, Lila tried getting out cereal for herself but grabbed the bag upside down and dumped granola all over my freshly mopped floor. Praying for wisdom and patience in these moments is paramount to sound, teachable opportunities. I let out a gasp but held back frustration as I flipped the bag over and calmly explained why the cereal dumped out. Instead of her crying from my yelling scaring her (which even just a few years ago or on a bad day right now would have been my response), she saw me helping her and said, "Me help cereal back" and started grabbing handfuls of cereal and stuffing them back into the bag. Mind you, the floor had just been mopped and protein granola cereal is expensive, so I let her stuff as much as her little, puffy toddler hands could put back in the bag and placed it right back on the pantry shelf before sweeping up the rest.

We don't have to be perfect, but we must not stay stagnant. The Lord said, "My grace is sufficient for you, for my power is made perfect in weakness" (2 Corinthians 12:9b). In our imperfections, He does his greatest work. He does this so we can boast that the changing power of the Lord is the only thing to explain our successes. If we aren't growing in our relationship with our Creator, then we are shortchanging our ability to thrive. Thriving plants grow; withering plants die. There is no in between.

We are all imperfect people interacting in relationships with other imperfect people. But, the Lord wants both parties in a relationship to continue to grow more in love and respect for one another as they grasp the depth of His love and sacrifice for each of them. If you are in a relationship that doesn't feel like it is thriving or are stuck in an abusive cycle, seek help. One marker for identifying relationships plagued with physical and emotional abuse are two-faced apologies. Making the victim feel personally responsible for the actions and words inflicted on them is pure manipulation, as the abuser convinces the victim that their behavior is what drove them to commit heinous acts. If this sounds like your situation, pray for wisdom, guidance, and safety in seeking help. The Lord is the giver of wisdom and patience and peace. He desperately wants us so grounded in His love and acceptance of us that no one can ruffle our feathers enough to steer us away from His peace that surpasses understanding.

Thankfully, Jesus came to Earth and lived the perfect life we could never live and died the death we all deserved so we don't have to. He took the pressure off of us to be perfect. He made communicating with our Heavenly Father possible so we can continue to grow in His love and use His power in place of our weakness. Start asking for those resources to flow into your heart today.

➡ **Jump to pages 112-116 in the Full Hands, Full Life Activity Companion Guide for this week's interactive prompts.**

Week 20: Stay Focused

Congratulations! You've made it to the halfway point in this transformational journey. If you were on a walk, this would be the point in your walk where you would turn around and start heading back. With every step, you are getting closer to your celebratory finish line.

In the next quarter, we will turn our attention outward—towards others. Focusing on relationships with others means focusing on things that are oftentimes out of our control. For some, getting out of our own heads will be a relief. For others, it will be scary. It is important to take time in the last week of this quarter to reflect on the rhythms you have enjoyed incorporating into your life the most and armor up for the road ahead.

Life is a series of small, seemingly inconsequential, choices that we make. The multitude of decisions we make increases as our level of responsibility increases. It's estimated that the average adult makes 35,000 remotely conscious decisions each day. Whether it's deciding to sleep in or get up early, or to slam on the brakes or hit the gas to fly through a yellow light, the weight of each decision on our future is not felt in the moment but can quickly add up to change the trajectory of our lives.

It's no surprise that gyms show sizable increases in new gym memberships in the months of January and May. New Year's resolutions and the impending swimsuit weather get people hyper-focused on their health goals. The same rings true for all types of life goals; if we associate a time frame with our goals, we are far more likely to keep the goals a priority.

When we know where we want to end up and when, the framework exists to guide those daily choices to move in that direction. After all, you can't get to where you want to be in five years if you don't start taking steps towards it now.

Early on in our marriage, my father-in-law encouraged Chris and I to keep at least one short term goal and one long term goal in front of our eyes at all times—anything from saving for a family day trip together or being able to purchase a home. He cautioned us that if we don't have some goals we are actively working towards together, then we could lose our connection as teammates in the game of life by getting caught up in the mundane day-to-day of parenting and work responsibilities. Keeping exciting goals in our periphery helps us maintain a healthy perspective on the day-to-day busyness playing a part in the success of a future goal.

I've enjoyed this practice so much that I consistently set goals in my life and write them down. For my ministry, we are asked to write two spiritual, personal, and ministry goals each semester. Spiritual goals could be spending quiet time with the Lord each morning or committing to attend a local church. Personal goals may include committing to working out a certain number of days a week or prioritizing sleep by setting a "nighty night" alarm on the phone. Ministry goals could include setting calendars and plans in advance making delegation possible or leading a Bible study for a group of leaders. At the start of the next semester, we review the goals. However, if those goals are not written down and in front of my eyes throughout the semester, I could blink, and it would be review time! Life travels fast if we aren't intentional in breaking down goals into manageable pieces. There is such a reward in seeing how achieving the goals allowed the Lord to work through the day-to-day moments.

For our family, we set goals for fun adventures together. We find that in the final weeks leading up to our vacations or rewards, we gain momentum to finish strong. However, with a goal in mind, it makes for tough choices along the way. To achieve a larger financial goal in the future, you may have to make smaller sacrifices along the way. For instance, to splurge on a plane ticket for an upcoming trip, you elect to skip the daily coffee shop line and make your coffees at home—taking more time and making more dishes, but saving $300 in a few short months.

Just the other week, the local fair was put up in the mall parking lot. The dazzling lights and spinning rides lit up the night sky as we drove by. The whole van erupted into shrieks of excitement from the youngsters while the older ones started reasoning why we should go. "It's back!" "We don't have anything going on!" "That looks bigger than last year's!" "It might be the last night!" But we as a family set a goal to go to the State Fair in the fall together—all eight of us—and each kid is saving to get the all-day ride passes for our time together. At that moment I wanted to say, "Yes, but just one ride!," which I knew would be impossible to achieve. Plus, Chris wasn't with us. However, having the goal to attend the massive 344 acre North Carolina State Fair already in motion with the kids saving chore money for their bands helped them rationalize without the whining that waiting was worth it.

This fair incident is no different than worldly temptations.

In his letter to the Romans, Paul urges them:

> *"Do not be conformed to this world, but be transformed by the renewal of your mind, that by testing you may discern what is the will of God, what is good and acceptable and perfect."*
> Romans 12:2 (ESV)

If we conform to valuing what the world commercializes as important, we are no better at finding direction than a ship lost at sea. When we see targeted ads in social media for things we want to buy or our kids ask for a special dessert during the week, without a goal in mind, the answer would easily be "yes." Saying "no" to yourself is hard enough, but saying "no" to a precious, five year old who is batting her lashes and looking up at you with her big, blue eyes is nearly impossible. We want to buy all the things and do all the fun activities. We don't enjoy playing Scrooge.

By constant renewal of our mind, including being in the Word, attending a Gospel-centered church, and getting into a small group of fellow believers to encourage one another, we will be able to hold up opportunities and temptations that come our way to what the Lord shows is good, acceptable, and perfect. If an opportunity isn't for me and is just a shiny distraction, then I want to know it before it is too late.

When it comes to staying future focused, we must consider not only what exists in plain sight, but also the goals and dreams we imagine our future holds. The two form a tangled web. Vision boards, a collection of images, objects, and/or words that exemplify your goals and dreams can do just that by creating a tangible representation of intangible items. Vision boards become a foundational reference point from where you launch towards achieving your goals and manifesting your dreams. Available in print or digital forms, their accessibility make them a valuable tool for any age with any budget. From creating vision boards on a piece of cardboard with old magazine pictures to elegant, frameworthy mosaics, the end results vary greatly. My children enjoy creating their own poster vision boards at the beginning of each year to help them weigh decisions in time management and pursue goals throughout the year.

Having a baby does not have to end your life's goals and dreams. If anything, it should multiply your dreams for a future not only for yourself, but a future of provision and opportunity for your little blessing alongside you.

Michael Ditton, an entrepreneur, author, and goal setting guru created the website goalsettingbasics.com to help people succeed in life by setting goals. After wanting to sail around the world, he set a five year goal to do just that, and seven years later was accomplishing that major feat as one of the youngest sailors in open water. He states that "fear is often a cause of failing to meet our goals. If we face fear, we stand a much better chance of conquering that fear and accomplishing our goals."[18] From that stance, he created an exclusive F.A.C.E.F.E.A.R. goal setting worksheet which I've included a link to in this week's Future Dreaming Activity. I use this particular worksheet in our mentor program to help moms set Financial, Attitude, Career, Education, Family, Exercise, Arts, and Recreation goals for them to set a path towards success. I hope it will be a helpful tool for you as well.

Your renewed mindset has the ability to become your new regular outlook. We are halfway through this creative, interactive, Scriptural guidebook, so I hope the momentum you've begun experiencing towards full life propels you with purpose into the second half of our journey together. Your future awaits!

➡ Jump to pages 118-122 in the Full Hands, Full Life Activity Companion Guide for this week's interactive prompts.

Weeks 21-30
Censoring Influencers

Full Hands, Full Life

Week 21: Find Your People

Well done, friend. Welcome to the second half of this experiential journey together. As they say, anyone can start something, but only those truly devoted and disciplined will finish it. You are showing your fortitude and strength to finish what you start. The euphoria of completing one task gives you confidence to complete the next, and that success will echo on into your future. Let's continue with this momentum as we jump into quarter three-focusing on others.

Have you ever heard the following quote attributed to motivational speaker, Jim Rohn?

"You're the average of the five people you spend the most time with."[19]

The idea is the people we surround ourselves with undoubtedly have a significant impact on our thoughts, behaviors, and who we become. Their impact can bleed into our way of thinking, our self-esteem, and our decision making. Being surrounded by positive, self-motivated people can cause their energy to rub off on us, inspiring us to achieve our goals.

On the other hand, if we surround ourselves with 'Debbie Downers' who lack self-control, we may see the glass of life half full and not worthy of putting forth effort to grow.

Last week we alluded to a key part in the continual renewal of your mind being the importance of finding a group of fellow believers who you can do life with. Many churches have small groups or community groups, who meet on a consistent basis together. Typically there is a person whose role at the church is connecting new believers or new church attendees to groups that will be a good fit for them (i.e. similar stages in life or interests). These small groups of people study scripture together, pray together, and share life victories and tragedies together, all in an effort to make the messiness of the world we live in less daunting than going through it alone.

Getting involved in a small group can be scary for some, especially those who have experienced hurt and pain from churches before. Sadly, churches are run by sinful people, since we are all sinful people. We all fall short of the glory of God, and yes, people in churches can sometimes cause undue pain on others. However, that will not be the experience in all churches! I can attest to that.

Chris and I have learned the importance of being part of a small group our entire married life. We value the time together with other believers in similar life stages, who share insights on how the Holy Spirit is unveiling and interpreting Scripture to them in remarkable ways. Not only that, we get to share and learn parenting wins together. We always leave our Wednesday community group study nights uplifted and encouraged. Not because we bring something special to the group, but because we leave knowing we aren't alone in what we are walking through. There are times when we can't see the Lord specifically moving in our lives. Questions are still unanswered. Doubts begin to surface. Yet in the middle of our community group, when a couple shares how a family member we've been praying for has been healed, a new job offers the exact raise needed for increased costs coming a family's way, or a wayward student in the classroom finds the Lord in the most unexpected circumstance, we are reminded of His presence. When you can't seem to find the Lord moving in your life, a shared sense of awe and wonder of His power surfaces when you see your Heavenly Father undeniably moving in the lives of those around you, reigniting a sense of peace and belief in your heart.

As a mother, I leave our small group re-fueled to enter my home and love on my kids. Just a few weeks ago we traveled with fourteen other families we've gotten to know through church small groups over the years to a family camp in Colorado. On the last night of the trip, the parents sat around a campfire and were posed a question by one of our trip leaders. He asked each person to share about someone they were thankful they were able to get to know better and were blessed to have on the trip. Chris and I had tears streaming down our cheeks as these friends shared how interactions with our children made such a positive impact on their own family's trip experience. Had we not opened our family up to form lifelong friendships, we would have missed out on the encouragement the Lord had in store for us that night.

Life is meant to be lived in community. That's why, as we discussed in Week 9, when the Lord looked at Adam, He knew life for him wasn't complete yet and created Eve. Choosing the right community makes all the difference. The Bible warns us by saying, "bad company corrupts good character" (1 Corinthians 15:33). Looking back over my college years, I would say, more times than I'd like to admit, I was the bad company others were seeking that ultimately corrupted their good character. Was I a bad person? Was I trying to lead others towards corruption? No and no. I was looking for a good time and looking for others to share those times with. However, my compass directing me towards a good time was pointing towards what the world's standard said was north! We've likely all played that role at some time or another.

Our role as a woman should look different when living from a Biblical perspective instead of a worldly one. When a group of women are chit chatting and the conversation turns to sharing their pet peeves of their husbands or boyfriends, our natural worldly instinct becomes longing to fit in. A desire to belong takes over. We feel the need to contribute our discontentment in order to empathize with them. But from a Biblical standpoint, these annoyances would serve us better to talk with our partner directly, instead of voicing them in the presence of others. It is remarkably easier to jump on the bandwagon and think of the things which annoy us about others, because this is the pattern of the world we live in. It is much harder to think about and share things about others that are pleasing to us or to steer the conversation in a more positive light.

Another prime example is when something goes wrong in our day. When someone asks, "How has your day been?," the things that instantly come to mind are the crazy traffic on the way to work, the coffee spilling in the car, the baby's blowout diaper on the carseat, or finding the last dozen eggs your helpful five-year-old put away while unloading the groceries in the freezer (yes, that one literally just happened at the time of writing this!). Being a positive light all around you is exhausting work. It is also impossible to achieve. We all need a safe group of people who can see us through our worst but have earned the right to encourage us out of our slumps.

How can we find good company? Start taking inventory of those you spend the majority of your time with. How do you feel after spending time with these people? Are you uplifted, feeling like you are ready to tackle the rest of the day with fervor? Or are you ready to take a nap, feeling exhausted from their conversations? Are you hanging out with people who you aspire to be like in five years? Or are you spending more time with people who, if given the choice, you would outgrow and mature beyond in your near future?

Censoring Influencers

After pondering these questions, you may have a better pulse on whether or not you are in the market for finding your people. The Lord did not make you the one human in the entire span of human existence He intended for isolation. He has created people you can pour into who are also able to pour back into your life. My prayer is that you will find other Christian friends who are looking for the same community you long for. You will be an answer to prayer for each other, which is a stellar place to start when forming a group of friends.

➡️ **Jump to pages 124-128 in the Full Hands, Full Life Activity Companion Guide for this week's interactive prompts.**

Full Hands, Full Life

Week 22: Advocate with Doctors

I've played piano since I was five years old. I mean I really played piano–in competitions, at church, for my middle and high school choirs. What you may not know is why I started playing piano.

Turning five was a major milestone in my childhood home. It was the launching point into your childhood sport of choice. My sister, Erin, who is 103 weeks older than me, which is one week shy of two years, knew she wanted to ride horses before she could even walk. While jumping in a bouncer saying, "jumping high, jumping fast," my mom made a promise that if Erin still wanted to jump high and fast when she turned five, she would take her horseback riding. One week after my third birthday when Erin turned five, we headed to a horse farm. Erin loved every second of it, but our birthdays are in February, and I was a sickly child. So, I promptly got sick from all the fresh barn air. My mom took me to get my throat checked, and the doctor said, "Well, you're getting a three for one today! We'll go ahead and treat her double ear infection with that strep throat!"

I stayed sick. For my fifth birthday, my mom begged

a piano teacher to start lessons for me to provide a mentally challenging indoor "sport." Now, this all sounds pretty sad and is making me out to be the sheltered, nerdy, scared-of-the-sun type of kid, but one fall a couple years later, my life changed drastically. For months, my doctor had been on a weekly retainer. At one visit, I consecutively had a double ear infection, bronchitis, mononucleosis, and impetigo.

    Maybe you've heard of a few of those, but the worst was impetigo because the skin surrounding your entire mouth displays a rash that looks like you're wearing bright red, clown lipstick. I remember I had to go to my mom's hairdresser appointment, which meant sitting for hours waiting for her perm to set. I slumped down in a waiting room chair with the same InStyle Hair magazine in front of my face for so long that my arms went numb. I didn't want anyone to see me. I was ashamed and embarrassed.

    My mom, recognizing the emotional havoc the back to back illnesses were taking on my socialization and ability to thrive in school, took action. My parents visited pediatrician after pediatrician to find one who recommended a dual tonsillectomy and adenoidectomy. The final pediatrician agreed the surgery would help me regain health, but there was a catch. For him to agree to refer me, I had to stay well. I hadn't been well in ten months! My mom found an outpatient surgery center, presented the case herself, and got the surgery approved. A couple weeks and a few gallons of ice cream later, my life started over again. I fell in love with horses and kept my love for piano. My ability to be a kid only came to fruition because of my mom's determination to be my health advocate.

    Being a health advocate for ourselves and those under our care is vitally important. However, I'm not advocating for using Google searches as your primary care physician Google health symptoms with utmost caution; worst case scenarios and outcomes pop up first because they get the most attention and clicks. Undue stress, incorrect diagnoses, and faulty self-medicating can all exacerbate health problems. Be willing to seek second opinions if something does not seem right. Exercise the right to change doctors if you feel like it is not going to work with one. Understand the time you spend in the doctor's office is your time.

When heading in for checkups with your children, here are a few suggestions I've found to make our appointments more efficient:

1. Be prepared to ask questions – Jot them down in the notes section of your phone when you think of them. Your doctor should be the best resource for an answer tailored to you or your children.

2. Take a video – If there is a troublesome behavior your child is exhibiting at home, record a video while they are in the comfort of their own home. Many times parents show up and try to explain a "tick" their child has, but the child will not cooperate and show the doctor due to the nerves in unfamiliar surroundings.

3. Call the nurse's line – If something does not feel right, feels off, or simply worries you, don't hesitate to call the nurses line. Many times they will answer whether you will need to go directly to the Urgent Care, ER, or simply come in to see a doctor. Other times, they save you the visit and give home remedy options.

Given all the advances in healthcare we've seen in the last century, am I alone in feeling shocked when a patient's symptoms still manage to baffle doctors? How humbling it must be to a medical professional, who is sought after for all the answers to admit they just don't know. Those same feelings of humility and bewilderment were shared by doctors during Jesus's time. In fact, Jesus was able to heal hundreds if not thousands of those who doctors cast aside as incurable–lepers, and the demon possessed, crippled, and paralyzed. In one such case, a woman is the recipient of a remarkable healing. Mark's gospel gives context clues around her battle through treatments during a condition of bleeding for twelve years:

> *"She had suffered a great deal under the care of many doctors and had spent all she had, yet instead of getting better she got worse."*
> Mark 5:26

How defeating! The part of her predicament that brings me to tears is the isolation she felt year after year. See, the cultural norm during that time was to see bleeding as unfit for society. During their monthly cycle, women would flee to the outskirts of the city gates and only return when bleeding had subsided. This rang true for all blood. So for twelve years, this woman had been shunned from society. With an incurable condition of this nature, which took her to every doctor within reach, the entire community knew of her ailment. She was an outcast-rejected. Even her own family disowned her in fear of the ailment making others view them as sub-par citizens. But during this story in Mark, she exemplified an incredible amount of bravery and advocacy for her health.

When the woman heard this man, the one they called Jesus, entered town, her mind started churning. Perhaps she overheard stories of Him healing the sick and the lame from neighboring towns. Maybe she thought, "Why not me? I've tried everything else. I have nothing more to lose. Life couldn't get any worse." So she mustered up enough courageous hope to brave the crowds she was forbidden to be in and crept closer and closer to Jesus. With disciples pushing back the crowds all around Him, without trying to cause a scene or bring any attention to herself, she reached out and grazed the edge of his cloak before seeping back into the shadows of the crowd.

Unbeknownst to her, Jesus felt His healing power leave. He knew she received the healing she desired but acknowledged the condition of her heart needing healing more than her body. She needed restoration.

Jesus sees our souls, not just our outward appearance or the inner workings of our bodies. So this interaction between the two continues with:

"At once Jesus realized that power had gone out from him. He turned around in the crowd and asked, 'Who touched my clothes?'

'You see the people crowding against you,' his disciples answered, 'and yet you can ask, 'Who touched me?'

But Jesus kept looking around to see who had done it. Then the woman, knowing what had happened to her, came and fell at his feet and, trembling with fear, told him the whole truth. He said to her, 'Daughter, your faith has healed you. Go in peace and be freed from your suffering.'"
Mark 5:30-34

Jesus wanted to call her out of the shadows but not to embarrass her—He knew full well she had experienced her fair share of embarrassment over the last decade—but to restore her. He called her daughter, perhaps a title she had longed to hear for years. He claimed her as His own, as part of His family. He desperately wanted to praise her courageous faith. He propelled her, with a crowd of witnesses to attest to it, to move on from her ailment to full life. Beyond her wildest dreams, she never foresaw this outcome, a life back in society. What a testimony she then had to share with all those with ears to listen!

My hope is that you will feel encouraged by this story in two ways. First, don't discount those feelings of "something's not quite right." Mother's intuition plays a large role in assessing the day-to-day wellbeing of our own children. Also remember that Jesus is in the business of life healing. He is Jehovah Rapha, the God who heals. He delights in healing our hearts and filling them with His Holy

Spirit to call us into full life. If you feel something keeping you from that, share it with Him. Be honest! He can handle it and will do so with grace.

➡️ **Jump to pages 130-134 in the Full Hands, Full Life Activity Companion Guide for this week's interactive prompts.**

Week 23: Minimizing Sibling Rivalry

Let's face it. Children develop entitlement syndrome far too early in life. You recognize it when you see it—that sense of entitlement or being owed a favor when nothing has been done to deserve special treatment-like jerking a toy out of a friend's hands, throwing their meal on the floor because dessert comes to the table, crying when they aren't allowed to do what the big kids do (the danger of said activity could easily end their life, but they don't see it that way!)

Shockingly enough, researchers say they don't know how this trait develops, but I'll tell you first hand it shows up without prompting at a very young age. Take Christmas at our home, for instance. After one Christmas blunder—naively thinking one of our littles was too little to notice the discrepancy—my husband and I now make every effort to wrap the same number of presents for each of our six children under the tree each year. Some presents contain multiple items and some items end up addressed to "Juengel Kiddos," but when we complete the unwrapping around the living room, everyone unwraps their last present at the same time. The justice in having an equal number of presents to unwrap supersedes the size of the boxes or the cost of items inside.

Over the last decade and a half, the ticket price on the wish list for Santa grew exponentially with the age of the children. We never sat our kids down and explained that no one else was looking out for them, so it was up to each to demand certain rights. The "me, myself, and I" tendency naturally developed on its own. The Christmas present balancing act got even trickier as we hosted foreign exchange students in our home for four years. These high school students became family. Like all other children, they desired to take part in the Christian tradition of opening gifts to celebrate Jesus' birth, so Chris and I brainstormed gifts to delight them on Christmas morning as well. Again, a natural tendency to show equal love to all the children in an attempt to minimize sibling rivalry.

For my type A personality, the quantifiable balance at Christmas feels right, but other aspects of sibling rivalry aren't as clear cut. Some children are talented in ways others are not. Some kids wish their sets of skills were more like another's. Some little ones despise the qualities they were blessed with all together and desperately desire to trade them in for a new set. Calling out and speaking about the attributes we see in our children is paramount to avoiding sibling rivalry, but we have to be diligent to balance even our praise around. A few of our children are naturally more prone to complete helpful tasks unprompted, while others are quiet comforters in tense situations. Their presence is felt by a calmness or a joy that fills the space, without them saying or doing anything noteworthy. Those quiet instances can often go unthanked.

At the end of the day, as we are putting our children down for the night, I love to recap the day with each of them. Many times I pose a question like:

* What was your favorite moment today?
* What made you laugh today?
* Who were you able to help today?

Then I use their responses to help frame a compliment on their character traits I see growing and developing in them. If something worthy of praise stuck out to me during the day and busyness distracted me from sharing it with them, I use this time to encourage them with it. This sweet time helps end what may have been a struggle bus kind of day on many fronts in a positive light.

Thankfully, sibling rivalry does not rear its ugly head in our home very often. From the beginning, Chris and I tried our darndest to grow excitement in our littles over new babies joining our family. While pregnant, we read books with Brooks highlighting the excitement of being a big brother. We let him listen to the baby's heartbeat on the doppler and feel her kicking in my tummy. We showed him the ultrasound pictures and explained how we knew what a good big brother he was going to be. Once the baby arrived, we found ways for him, even at two years old, to play major roles in the care of his baby sister, Ellie. I strategically placed baby care items on a level he could reach—think unbreakable ones like diapers, wipes, burp cloths, or rattles. He proudly toddled over to retrieve these items when prompted. We let him introduce her or "show off his baby" to people who came over. I taught him how to hold her and burp her, telling him how much she loved watching him make funny faces at her and how her eyes lit up the second the sound of his voice entered the room. When she started eating baby food, we waited for him to be home to share in that moment. When she got close to taking her first steps, we let him hold her hands to help her "work out" and get stronger leg muscles. Looking back now I see it was a risk, but a toddler helping a baby walk was just too darn cute to pass up!

These shared affection-growing moments continued with each additional child. By the time we had our fourth, our older kids (ages six, four, and two at the time) could warm bottles, change diapers, pick out baby outfits, bathe and even swaddle the newest addition. Not because they HAD to, but because they enjoyed holding such important roles in the lives of their new siblings. They felt needed, not forgotten. They complimented each other on how careful and talented they were at settling down the upset baby.

Do I think sibling rivalry won't happen if families use these tactics? Not necessarily, but I do feel like implementing some of these strategies and being mindful of making children in the home feel they have a significant role to play makes a positive difference. Our children level up each time we have another child; they aren't demoted. Thankfully they have risen to the occasion each and every time.

I still feel the parental guilt over not carving out enough one-on-one time with each individual child. I stress over doing things equally for each that financially may not be the wisest choice. I desire each to experience their own giftings instead of being lumped together into one focus because they share the same last name, so if that means we are dabbling in piano, choir, crochet, basketball, karate, drums, babysitting, sign language, horseback riding, and every genre of dance under the sun in the same calendar year, so be it. The sacrifices in our schedules, finances, and sheer exhaustion today are more than paid back in full getting to see our children hone in on the giftings the Lord knit into the very fabric of their lives.

We tell our kids often that they need to be each other's biggest cheerleaders. Friends will come and go, but family is forever. The Bible speaks to this in an often misunderstood verse in Proverbs:

A friend loves at all times, and a brother is born for a time of adversity.
Proverbs 17:17

Being siblings is a deeper bond than friendships. Though friends may love you through the good and bad, many friends won't go to battle with you. When everyone else turns their back, your siblings are the ones that rush in with battle armor, reinforcements, and encouragement.

Censoring Influencers

They ought to be the ones reminding you what you are truly made of. They remember the times you've overcome and speak life into you. Treating siblings with that mindset puts the day-to-day bickering in its rightful place. Although it is a morbid thought, we pray our children will have each other as a support system long after Chris and I are gone. It is our duty now to build up a strong love for each other to withstand whatever life throws their way. Together we are stronger. Building each other up in the company of others—friends, co-workers, strangers— speaks volumes to our loyalty to one another. Ecclesiastes 4:12 (ESV) says, "And though a man might prevail against one who is alone, two will withstand him—a threefold cord is not quickly broken." If a threefold cord is not quickly broken, then a sixfold rope must be impenetrable!

This may not be the type of sibling relationship you experienced growing up. Perhaps there is a strained relationship now with your own siblings, or with siblings from previous relationships and blended families. I am a firm believer it is never too late to start mending bridges, but first, pray to ask for guidance on how the bridge can be built. Pray to ask if a bridge should be built. Ask for your heart to be in the right place to do the work, as far as you are able, to make these relationships thrive. Start finding ways to praise even the little ways that you see improvements or glimpses of healthy heart posture changes towards redemption. Above all else, know you are adopted into the family of God. You are a child of God, beloved, and have an inheritance in the family where you belong. May your children experience family bonds that are an impenetrable cord which holds fast through any storm. May your confidence in the truth of your belonging grow from this point forward.

➡️ **Jump to pages 136-140 in the Full Hands, Full Life Activity Companion Guide for this week's interactive prompts.**

Week 24: Fleeing Generational Curses

Take a moment and ponder things your parents did that made you cringe inside. It's ok, we've all had these thoughts. What about them embarrassed you in front of your peers? What made you want to crawl under a table and disappear? For some, this list may have one undeniable, glaring answer. For others, the list may be unending. Sadly, if left unchecked, we are more likely to implore the same parenting style we experienced than not.

My parents were both incredibly supportive. They showed up at all my extracurriculars and encouraged me to strive for excellence, so these next two stories might pale in comparison to your experience. The first is such a little thing, I hesitate to share it, but it is such a great example of a parent doing something for our benefit repetitively that kids still find it cringeworthy. My mom used to clean food off my chin by licking her finger and scrubbing the mess of my face. Usually, this was first thing in the morning on the way out of the house, meaning I could smell her coffee and creamer well into the first hour of the school day. Had I voiced my disapproval, my loving mother would have gladly taken the extra second to wet a paper towel and scrub my face, but I have no memory of sharing how much I loathed her habit. When my kids inevitably started needing a face clean while we dashed out the door, I changed it up a bit. I ask them to lick their finger, which I then use to tidy up their mouth. Is it better? Probably not, but hopefully it is a step in the right direction.

Now my dad's moment was a one and done kind of memory. On one particular evening, I remember announcing a boy who was interested in me was stopping by the house. That very evening, my Dad decided it was the right time to lay his hunting gear out on the kitchen counter for a cleaning. I don't remember ever seeing that paraphernalia any other time in my life, although my Dad took a yearly hunting trip. Coincidence? I think not! My dad likely saw red flags in that relationship that I never detected. Needless to say, the guy never came back. Yet, when I brought Chris home the first time, I joked with my dad that the hunting gear was not necessary this time because a worthy suitor would be approaching the door.

Maybe your cringeworthy moments are harder to share. Maybe they became a regular occurrence in your home life or are something which have plagued your family for generations, like violence, generational trauma, addiction, codependency, hoarding, poverty mindset, single parenthood, promiscuity, gambling, or toxic parenting habits. However, for a generational curse to be lifted, it only takes one generation to stand up against the status quo and turn the ship around.

I share the following with permission from both of our fathers and with utmost respect for the tough day-in and day-out choices our fathers had to make so we did not have to battle this demon in our own lives. Both of our paternal grandfathers held an unhealthy, addictive relationship with alcohol. The Los Angeles County Department of Mental Health website shares that "Many scientific studies, including research conducted among twins and children of alcoholics, have shown that genetic factors influence alcoholism. These findings show that children of alcoholics are about four times more likely than the general population to develop alcohol problems."20 Both of our dads stood firm and made the choice, day after day, to not succumb to the natural desire to give in to alcohol. Because of their strength, Chris and I did not have the cards stacked against us when it came to alcohol. We had and still have other challenges we are battling but not that particular one, and for that, we are forever grateful.

What if you became the generation to stand up and make a change for your children? When it comes to choosing something which goes against my nature, if it is in favor of my kids, the answer will always be "yes." Let me give you an example. If Chris and I are watching TV, and I see a spider on the ceiling, my natural instinct is to squeal and beg him to go kill it. I don't want anything to do with the bugs, even those that only crawl and pose no threat to me if I squish them with my bare hands. The same is true if Brooks is within earshot. I'm not going to electively trap and release the skink or lizard back into the wild that makes its way inside. I'm jumping on a chair begging Brooks to come in and take care of business, which he does every time without murmuring a complaint—thank you, Brooks! Now, if it's me and my girls in the vicinity, and they're screeching and crying big elephant tears down their cheeks, I muster up all the courage I've got and start slaying stink bugs, bees, snakes, or mice. Heck, one time even a cicada-sized killer wasp made its way into our Barbie house, and I had my flip flop in hand swatting before it hit Skipper's bedroom floor!

Bottom line, when you don't feel you have enough strength, look into the eyes of your kids. I promise you can stand in the gap for your kids easier than you can stand in it for yourself. That's the way the Lord made us.

Therefore, if anyone is in Christ, he is a new creation. The old has passed away; behold, the new has come.
2 Corinthians 5:17 (ESV)

When we are born again by accepting Jesus as our Lord and savior over our life, our old life passes away.

Our new life is born. This is called our second birth. We are no longer defined by our past failures. Our future is not dependent on our past. We are promised a new life. A renewed sense of purpose. We no longer have to hide behind or fall in line with the norms of past generations in our family tree. We get a fresh new start.

Perhaps your family's generational curses like overworking, unforgiveness, laziness, anger, or addiction caused them to not show up at performances or games. Maybe they became unreliable or unable to offer safe rides to these events that you only became a part of to have an undeniable excuse to avoid going home after school. You rewrote in your mind that it was actually a good thing, even a blessing, they did not show up to embarrass you on the sidelines, but if you really look inwardly long enough, you know you always wanted them there. All the other parents were there cheering on their kids or hollering at them to move the ball, get in there, or be aggressive, which are tough things to hear, but they were there to celebrate those game winning goals, incredible assists, and "see the game" passes. Maybe, just maybe, if your parents had been on the sidelines, they would have seen something in you that they had never seen before, become proud of you in a way you never thought possible, or even been driven to step up their parenting game and value you because of your skill that allowed them to beam with pride. Through years of mentoring adolescent parents whose own parents were absent in their lives, I've watched the beauty unfold as they describe a clear picture of what they don't want their own parenting style to look like. From there they start writing their own story of who they want to become as a parent.

Along this book writing journey, a sweet friend encouraged me more than she will ever know with her words: "Don't waste your story." We are created as new in Christ Jesus, but our memories are not wiped clean. We can glean from our pasts and move forward into new light. The beauty in being able to see glaring holes in your parents' parenting style is the ability to articulate what you don't want to emulate. From there, you can start describing what you want your parenting style to be remembered as in the light of your new life. Welcome to your invitation to embrace this journey. After all, you were hand picked for such a time as this!

➡ **Jump to pages 142-146 in the Full Hands, Full Life Activity Companion Guide for this week's interactive prompts.**

Full Hands, Full Life

Week 25: Forgiving the Un-forget-able

"Forgiveness is made for the one who's been hurt." I heard this statement at a women's conference several years back. The words haunted me. How on Earth could they be true? How can humbling yourself enough to forgive someone who has caused you emotional, physical, or mental pain be a gift to yourself?

Let me try to explain by sharing a pivotal relationship in my life which brings up so many memories of shame and guilt in hopes that it brings you freedom to think through your relationships with a newfound honesty.

When I was in grade school, the North Carolina public school system mapped out districts based on neighborhood proximity to schools. Namely, all the kids in and around your home would attend the same elementary, middle, and high schools to maximize efficiency in the bus system. However, a particular magnet middle school across town focused on the arts. The surrounding neighborhoods were the district's neighborhoods for that school, but students from anywhere in the county could apply to be accepted into this school's "gifted & talented" program. As a budding pianist and labeled an "AIG" (Academically or Intellectually Gifted) student in elementary school, it made logical sense to apply to the "GT" (Gifted & Talented) arts middle school. Gaining entrance into that middle school was a highlight in my young life. It was a ticket to advance, stay challenged, and make my own path instead of following the trajectory set before me. My excitement over the change actually surprised me as I electively chose to start over with new friends and teachers, making a name for myself instead of continuing to middle school where my older sister already paved a solid path before me. While all my other friends from elementary school continued on together in our neighborhood middle school, I rode a different bus, which traveled much further and made my schedule completely different from theirs. We lost touch, and they developed deep friendships that our short, weekend time together couldn't hold a candle to. Thankfully, I also found friends, although most were on the other side of the city, making getting together outside of school far more logistically challenging than having friends right down the street.

When the decision to select a high school came around, I faced a familiar choice. Apply to the magnet high school (attending the magnet middle school nearly ensured my acceptance into the high school) or switch back to the public route. Although I wanted to carry my middle school friendships into high school, the bus ride to and from the magnet high school was going to add over two hours to the "school day." The prospect of the bus ride along with being reunited with my lifelong best friend, Kelly, who lived diagonally across the street from me for ten years, ultimately made my decision an easy one. Kelly and I were thrilled at the possibility of being at school together again. Kelly's kind, bubbly, and trustworthy demeanor made her a fast friend to everyone. I felt confident in her promise to introduce me to all her friends, which she did effortlessly! Unfortunately for me, I also sought after those familiar faces from elementary school who were now at my high school.

One person in particular ended up in nearly all of my classes freshman year. In elementary school, he was already known as a "bad boy," and I would fall victim to his brash words and coarse humor, which led to tears time and time again. Against all of Kelly's pleadings, as she had witnessed his reputation in middle school, I grew fond of his confident, borderline pushy advances.

Ladies, why are we sometimes attracted to the one thing with flashing neon lights all around it saying "caution," "dangerous," "dead end?" In this instance, he somehow managed to paint a picture in my mind of him being completely different from what people defined him as, and I electively put up blinders just long enough for him to become my boyfriend. I quickly found out why he was single and that I was just fresh meat for him. I ended our relationship abruptly but not soon enough. He spread rumors about me to the entire high school that affected the way I saw myself and set me on a path to prove all the rumors wrong. Sadly, they seemed so believable, my attempts to 'right' them proved futile. He continued on his path of destruction through the school, and I just became another byproduct and number of casualties caused by relationship with him.

Over the years, the sting of his words and memories of his actions have dulled, and the Lord has graciously given me the ability to forgive him. However, the retail space his words and actions took up in my mind can still rear their ugly head today. Even as I write, I feel my heartbeat quickening in my chest, as my mind remembers the trauma endured. Yet I am thankful for those moments in my life which led me to heed the Lord's divine, overabundant grace and mercy. In my quest for wholeness again, I began speaking the Bible verse, "You are precious in my eyes, and honored, and I love you" (Isaiah 43:4). The thought that the Lord of the universe finds me precious and honored still brings me to happy tears. You, fellow teammates in the third quarter of this game, are precious and honored daughters of the highest priest and creator of everything. He loves you.

It doesn't matter who says anything contradicting this statement. Synonyms for precious are worthy, valuable, admirable, and worthwhile. Let those be the first thoughts you speak in your mind and what comes out of your mouth this week. Our true Father sees us as precious, worthy, valuable, admirable, and worthwhile.

Out of the Lord's example of ultimate mercy for me by withholding deserved punishment for the wrongdoings in my life, I am able to extend the same mercy towards this high schooler from my past, but my heart races for other girls who fell into his path who have not gained the same viewpoint. How many others endured tarnished futures and still feel the pain of that burden today?

Hebrews 12:14-15 outlines how bitterness and seeds of unforgiveness take root. "Pursue peace with all people, and holiness, without which no one will see the Lord: looking carefully lest anyone fall short of the grace of God; lest any root of bitterness springing up, cause trouble, and by this many become defiled" (Hebrews 12:14-15 NKJV). In his book, The Bait of Satan: Living Free from the Deadly Trap of Offense, John Bevere says,

> "If roots are nursed—watered, protected, fed, and given attention—they increase in depth and strength If not dealt with quickly, roots are hard to pull up. The strength of the offense will continue to grow ... Now instead of the fruit of righteousness (love, joy, peace, patience, kindness, goodness, faithfulness, gentleness, and self-control) being produced, we will see a harvest of anger, resentment, jealousy, hatred, strife, and discord. Jesus called these evil fruits. (See Matthew 7:19-20)"[21]

One day we will all stand in front of our Creator and need to answer for our actions. That is a heavy thought, but we serve a just God. Are there relationships from your past that make it hard to move forward without glancing back and placing blame? Romans 12 tells us to, "Do all that you can to live in peace with everyone. Dear friends, never take revenge. Leave that to the righteous anger of God" (Romans 12:18-19). For years, I wanted this boy to get what he had coming to him. In the first few years, I wanted him to at least acknowledge what transpired between us. I held the root of bitterness in my heart for decades, but while reading John Bevere's aforementioned book, these words jumped off the page:

> "If Jesus had waited for us to come to Him and apologize, saying, 'We were wrong. You were right. Forgive us,' He would not have forgiven us from the cross. As He hung on the cross, He cried out, 'Father, forgive them, for they do not know what they do' (Luke 23:34). He forgave us before we came to Him confessing our offense against Him. We are admonished by the words of the apostle Paul: 'Even as Christ forgave you, so you also must do" (Col. 3:13). And 'be kind to one another, tenderhearted, forgiving one another, even as God in Christ forgave you" (Eph. 4:32)."

The Lord calls us to forgive so we can move forward. In Matthew 18, Jesus tells the parable of the unforgiving debtor. The King forgives his servant for a debt the equivalent of 75 pounds of gold or $4.5 billion in today's standards. That servant, quickly forgetting his own insurmountable debt that was forgiven, turns around and forces a fellow servant to repay him the equivalent of 100 days worth of wages. When this second servant begged the King's servant for mercy, the King's servant threw him in prison. Upon hearing the account of the servant's rage, the King turned him over to the jailors to be tortured until he could repay the full original, unpayable debt owed. Jesus then explains, "'This is how my heavenly Father will treat each of you unless you forgive your brother from your heart'" (Matthew 18:35).

The bitterness in my heart did not need to leave based on this high schooler's acknowledgement of wrongdoing or an apology. I needed to forgive him so I could move forward and not continue to carry the shame and weight of that time moving forward. But how?

The Lord prompted me to pray for him. Not shallow prayers, but the kind of prayers that come from the depths of the soul, like those I lift up for my own children. To pray for his deliverance from any unspoken guilt he has over those years of his past. To pray for Jesus to capture his heart in such a way that he starts finding ways to stand up for injustices like human trafficking plaguing our world today. It has been nearly two decades since our paths crossed and the prayers only started the past two months. Since praying, I have felt a release in my heart but a burden knowing he is still lost, succumbing to the patterns of this world. With a lightened heart I now thank the Lord for bringing me to the other side of the trials and tribulations.

The Apostle Peter wrote in 1 Peter 4:12-13, "Dear friends, don't be surprised at the fiery trials you are going through, as if something strange were happening to you. Instead, be very glad—for these trials make you partners with Christ in his suffering, so that you will have the wonderful joy of seeing his glory when it is revealed to all the world" (NLT). On this side of forgiveness, I now see I have experienced a victory which only came about through tragedy. I thank the Lord that through my story, your story may have a new, refreshed launching point of forgiveness. Let us encourage one another with our stories, for without them we couldn't be or become the mothers we are today.

➡ **Jump to pages 148-152 in the Full Hands, Full Life Activity Companion Guide for this week's interactive prompts.**

Week 26: Balancing Comparison

The quote, "Comparison is the thief of joy," attributed to Theodore Roosevelt, the 26th president of the United States, has gained massive relevance in our current social media era. Psychology Today research showed that more than 10% of daily thoughts involve making a comparison of some kind.[22] And with social media allowing us to only show our highlight reels, comparison seems unavoidable.

When Leighton, our second daughter, was young enough that we still kept track of how old she was in months, I remember Chris taking her on a grocery shopping trip with him. He proudly worked through her budding vocabulary as they walked up and down the aisles. "Milk." "Bread." He even got a few two-syllable words like "apple" and "yogurt" where an attuned parent ear would decipher the item but the unsuspecting bystander may only hear babbling. In the middle of this proud dad moment, another dad came around the turn of the aisle with his similarly-aged child going through a similar exercise. Except this child, when prompted, undeniably recited the spelling of "hippopotamus." This word is even tough for adults to say with clarity, let alone spell! For all Chris knows, that could have been the only word the child knew, but it was enough to knock him down a few notches.

Comparison, when left unchecked, can lead to poor mental health and incite anxiety and depression. In extreme cases, comparison can cause people to stop trying to achieve altogether. Thankfully, Chris and I did not let this grocery store, savant toddler show up our Leighton! Her cute little toddler voice was uttering "hip-poo-poo-toe-moose" in no time!

Although comparison can urge you to try new things and reach higher goals, the lure of comparison occurs for a variety of reasons. Sometimes it is to selfishly make ourselves feel better by pointing out another person's flaws. Other times we want to validate our position in life. However, to rid our lives of comparison altogether would likely lead to unmotivated, low-performing individuals, so what does a healthy comparison approach look like?

Thankfully, the Bible paints a clear picture on how to attack our natural strive towards "keeping up with the Joneses" while simultaneously keeping ourselves in check. In his letter to the church in Galatia, Paul wrote:

> *"Each one should test their own actions. Then they can take pride in themselves alone, without comparing themselves to someone else, for each one should carry their own load."*
> Galatians 6:4-5

If we are to test our own actions, that means we are to weigh our performance against our best effort. Did we do our best? When we do, we feel good about the results. There is no need to compare ourselves with others. When we are carrying our own load, then the load size is dependent on our ability, not the load size of others.

There is one person we should look at to compare our actions with, and that is Jesus. The examples of how He interacted with others and conducted His life inspire us to do our best. The way He loves us when we fall short on our responsibilities gives us comfort when we fail to capitalize on our opportunities. Yet, I constantly find myself comparing my life to others on social media. Can you relate?

Social media did not easily work itself into my normal routine. Personally I found myself exhausted trying to write the best captions or pair a clever hashtag with each Instagram or Facebook photo. Photos sat in draft status for far too long as interruptions pulled me away before choosing the best filter or clever caption. Everyone else seemed to manage their social accounts better than I ever could. I thought their content must effortlessly ooze from their fingertips! I held guilt over the multitude of moments I captured on my camera but failed to set aside time to post. My camera roll has about a hundred thousand pictures, but I feel this pressure to post only the most flattering pictures of my kids. I'll have to answer to them at some point on which ones I put out there for the world to see. Yet, with services that automatically print books from the pictures my husband and I post, I appreciate that a photo album shows up every so often from the time I do devote to the socials. So, my perspective had to shift. Either I let the comparison of others' perfectly captioned socials paralyze me from posting my own, or I truly post for the mailed albums that become a catalyst for conversation and joy in our living room.

Might I suggest that if social media is constantly causing you to compare yourself in a negative light to others, perhaps take a hiatus from it. Wait until the auto-response to pick up your phone when you have a moment of boredom to scroll dissipates before logging back in.

Comparison off-line is prevalent in social circles as well. One of my dear friends is gifted in all things sentimental. When her first daughter graduated high school, she opened her own copy of Dr. Seuss's *Oh the Places You Will Go*. The book itself is a staple at graduation ceremonies and parties, but her daughter's was special. For the past thirteen years, her mother had covertly acquired messages of encouragement and memories from teachers that sowed into the life of her daughter each year. In one sitting, her daughter was able to relive her life and decisions she made that culminated into high school graduation. In that instant, she was able to look around and lock eyes with dozens of the teachers and administrators who played formidable roles in this accomplishment. No one counted likes. No one compared pictures, but the sentiment rang loudly in her heart.

What I find most beautiful about our Heavenly Father is His ability to love us all completely, wholeheartedly, and fully. With six children, I only see a glimpse of this level of love in the way my heart's love capacity grew with each blessing we added to our family. Unlike our proverbial "love buckets," the Lord doesn't need us to work at filling His back up. His "love bucket" has an endless stream of water flowing into it that allows ours to be constantly filled from its overflow. You are already so important to the Lord. You can rest assured that when others make you feel less than, mediocre, or not good enough, you are already somebody special to the Lord. He loves you just the way you are. Let the confidence in that love help you grow into the nurturer that the Lord created you to be.

➡ Jump to pages 154-158 in the Full Hands, Full Life Activity Companion Guide for this week's interactive prompts.

Week 27: Managing Family Dynamics

I challenge you to find one person without a favorite "Uncle ..." or "Cousin ..." in their family. You know, the relatives you could tell some stories about, and either have friends rolling in laughter or crying out in disbelief. Perhaps that family member is a sibling, a parent, an in-law, or a distant cousin, uncle, or aunt. Whoever this individual may be in your life, they always bring a full range of emotions to mind when you find out they are coming to the family reunion or annual family vacation.

Growing up, my cousin Leigh Anne brought about that emotion in the best way. Her bright, blond hair and twinkly eyes lit up the room. She was about twenty years older than me, so in my eyes she always felt like a cool aunt. She had the most contagious laugh, told stories that kept you on the edge of your seat, and held a confident air about her that led you straight to trust. Her knack of finding the perfect gifts and never shying away from saying what the rest of us were thinking made her the life of family gatherings. Her twin brother, Dale, kept her in check, but also marveled at her effortless ability to move in and out of conversations from any room in the house. In many ways

I looked up to her and still do to this day. She and I held a special place in our grandmother's heart. Grandmama Wood was the only grandparent I knew growing up. My father's parents were gone before memories could form, and my mother's father passed before I was born, so Grandmama became solely responsible for all the memories I have of what a grandparent should be—and she did not disappoint! She spoiled me rotten, but I was far from her only grandchild. Both cousin Leigh Anne and I took every opportunity we could get to spend time with our grandmother, just decades apart. Leigh Anne would run away to Grandmama's in the 70s, with my visits taking place in the 90s. We'd snap green beans in the living room while watching her daily stories (daytime tv soap operas) and sip coke straight from the tiniest glass bottles that lived in the garage mini-fridge. As you'd imagine, due to my sans-caffeine home life, I could never finish a full mini-Coke, which made her chuckle and tell me to just slip it back in the fridge for later, which never arrived. We'd stay up late chatting about life happenings and dreaming of what my future would be like. Grandmama never hurried us along, content to be doing nothing if we were doing nothing together. As dementia and Alzheimer's started settling in, clouding memories in Grandmama's early nineties, I took it as a compliment when she started calling me Leigh Anne. I knew the affection the name held in her mind and felt honored to share in its place.

What I'd do to bring those Grandmama Wood family gatherings back—to let our kids get to know Grandmama the way I knew her, to watch Leigh Anne set everyone at ease with her inviting smile and her well-timed jokes, the tables lined with everyone's beautiful dishes, an entire table devoted to desserts like Grandmama's seven layer coconut cake or perfectly baked pecan pie, and sitting on the floor playing holiday music on a keyboard plugged into the hallway outlet because the end tables and coffee tables were expertly staged with trinkets and book displays. But time is fleeting and memories fade, so we move forward not to replace the people but in an effort to grow deep memories again with loved ones by our side.

For our children, these fond memories surround both sets of grandparents, which is a rare gift these days. Having loving, Christian grandparents, eager to help share in the rearing and forming of our children is something we never take for granted. We also continue to cultivate fond memories from holidays spent and trips experienced with Chris's side of the family. All of these relatives are such foundational role models in our children's lives, whom I hope they emulate in various ways as they grow and mature into adults.

If managing family dynamics in your life resembles mine, then you are stuck with the task of dividing up holidays, and figuring out which side of the family won't feel slighted if you celebrate a day early or a day late. You'll be stuck trying to remember which family gets Christmas or Thanksgiving that year, or if Easter is potentially a holiday both sides of the family can celebrate together. What a blessing.

But what happens when those close family members bring about a swirl of negative emotions? What if they hold the potential to be incredibly involved in the life of your child against your best wishes? Toxic relationships can do to a family what salt does to food—completely change the flavor.

My husband and I share the opinion that the best cookie we've ever found is the "Kitchen Sink" cookie from Panera. Large in size and flavor, this cookie packs a punch. From the perfect portion size (large enough to share), soft enough to warrant no re-heating, and thick enough to stay together when picked up to the perfect mix of sweet, savory, and salty—semi-sweet chocolate, milk chocolate, caramel pieces, and pretzels—the cookie boasts mere perfection. But the icing on the cake, if you will, are the visible flakes of salt resting on the top, which round out the flavor profile to a tee. Sometimes those family members with differing opinions or less than savory habits keep everyone else honest about seeing the other side of an argument. They keep everyone open to viewing social and political ideologies from another perspective, challenging them to have empathy with others leading to compassion and grace. But other times, the habits and tendencies of family members make us avoid the other side all together, keeping them rightfully at arms length. If the Panera baker mistakenly adds a cup of salt in place of the cup of sugar, both being similar in weight, color, and texture, the batch of Kitchen Sink cookies becomes inedible.

Do you see a division between you and family members because of how tainted your family's past is? In some situations, setting up boundaries to protect you and your children can be the healthiest decision you can make.

In Galatians, Paul, who was an apostle–or ambassador–for Jesus asked something I try to use as my barometer for life decisions: "For am I now seeking the approval of man, or of God? Or am I trying to please man?" (Galatians 1:10). In the height of his message spreading about the hope and true identity of Jesus as the Son of God and Savior of the world, Paul was wondering if he was spreading the message in a way to selfishly gain more friends or if he was being true to the calling on his life.

Family dynamic choices are much the same. Reframed, those verses could be read, "Are you simply going along with the status quo to avoid conflict, yet putting you and your children in compromising situations along the way?" The Lord has called us to care for, nurture, and protect our children to the best of their ability. That includes their well-being. That includes discerning the right voices to speak into their lives, the right adults to trust them with. Trying to please louder, stronger, or pushier family members while forsaking personal convictions poses a real threat to the health of each individual family unit.

What the Lord says about us in Isaiah 43:3, He says about our children as well:

Censoring Influencers

"...you are precious in my eyes, and honored, and I love you,..."
Isaiah 43:4 (ESV)

Creating space and putting in boundaries for ourselves for who we spend time with and when and how could be in your children's best interest. Pray for discernment in those relationships. Pray for the right way to establish healthy boundaries. Boundaries can be a lifeline, a means of regaining control from traumatic past experiences, and a path to genuine self-care. Boundaries need to be clear and communicated. They typically span four categories. Not all might pertain to your motherhood journey, but you may be shocked to find one resonating with you more than the others.

* Conversational Boundaries - limits to what topics we are open to discussing and what topics we do not feel comfortable talking about, especially around our children.
* Physical Boundaries - ones set for ourselves to ensure physical safety and proximity, including when and where we go places, whether or not our children go places, and what we are comfortable with physically from others.
* Time Boundaries - set to create a healthy mindset and schedule for ourselves, which can include setting limits on how much time we spend with someone or doing a certain activity and establishing work/school and home life balance.
* Relationship Boundaries - limits are discussed and agreed upon with your significant other, family, coworkers, and close friends.

Once we have boundaries defined, we then need to communicate them with the correct people. After the boundary has been communicated, if it is breached, then an appropriate response is warranted–perhaps time apart, another conversation, or in some cases legal action.

Boundaries differ from person to person and can change when growth is evident. If you are ready to start making your boundaries, start by setting one boundary with one person or activity. Keep establishing healthy boundaries until you feel you and your children are safe and comfortable in your daily walk as precious, honored, and loved children of the Lord.

➡ **Jump to pages 160-164 in the Full Hands, Full Life Activity Companion Guide for this week's interactive prompts.**

Week 28: Facing Comments from Others

Several months ago, a dear friend of mine experienced the loss of her mother. Her mother's health had been declining for some time so her passing was no surprise, but something shared at the funeral gave me a clear perspective on why the loss felt so heavy. Her mom, once a champion prayer warrior, cheerleader of a mother, and recipient of the gift of prophecy had her most treasured character trait—her gift of encouragement—stripped away for decades by the effects of a disease which plagued her body. She became irritable, unable to control her temper, and worse yet, unable to feel remorse for her actions. She lost the foundation of who she was, but in her final months, the kindness returned. The continual reminder of her love for her children through muddled words, hugs, and eye squinching smiles. The true fabric of her being returned after years of the family thinking they would never see it again. It was as if her internal turmoil came to rest as her body continued to fail. She regained control through extreme loss. As her mom danced through the pearly gates of Heaven, my friend grieved losing the sweet, caring version of her mother again. How trapped her mom must have felt all those years wanting to react one way, yet lacking control over her very arms, legs, and mouth to line up desire with reality.

As I sat in the pew with tears streaming down my cheeks, I saw the ability to choose kindness as a true gift for the first time. Even the ability to be kind can be stripped away, so why choose to treat others any other way? This was a true conviction of heart, because I have been known to have a short fuse. From haggling prices to my mama bear side puffing up at a moment's notice, I embarrassingly have put people in their place with my words more times than I can count. But after the adrenaline wears off from these situations, the ick feeling sets in.

The Bible warns us in Proverbs that, "Those who guard their lips preserve their lives, but those who speak rashly will come to ruin" (Proverbs 13:3). Not sure about you, but I choose a guarded life over ruin any day! So, why is it so easy to spout off when offended?

As I write, I'm still in the process of learning how to choose kindness in all situations, especially in the comfort of my own home, but perhaps you can relate on some level. If you are currently pregnant, or recently had a child, then you most definitely can relate to those hormones flooding through your veins right now. Maybe I should give a disclaimer here that this week's focus may spark some memories for you over past comments people have made.

After being pregnant six times, I've likely heard every inappropriate, anger invoking (I already admitted my internal struggle with being hot headed) "you're pregnant" comment from complete strangers multiple times. Why do strangers suddenly gain courage to share life wisdom when they see a pregnant woman approaching? Or, why do they feel we can take a backhanded compliment or subtle dig at life choices when we are raging hormone machines?

Let me also remind you that when I go into a store, I typically have a gaggle of kids around making us a walking circus act, which is open season for any and all judgmental comments. Now, I'm closer to the example setter on how not to react rather than how to respond based on my track record, but there have been moments I've seen the redemptive nature of the Lord in conversations. By sharing a few, I hope to rewrite your path forward with the unsolicited comments from family members, friends, and strangers at large.

Ladies, people say the darndest things. If they had a bad sleeper, they share, "You better sleep now cause you'll never sleep again." If you have children around, they say, "I guess you haven't figured out how this keeps happening yet." Some make judgements on the size of your family like, "This is your last one, right?" Or, "Those can't all be your kids." My least favorites were the ones that made you feel like a beached whale on a day you felt you actually looked pretty cute, "Wow, you've gotten so big!," "You must be expecting twins," or "How far past your due date are you?" Kids often aren't better! I remember heading out ten days post c-section with our third to Brooks's soccer game. One of his teammates who could not have been more than four at the time said, "Oh, I thought you already had your baby?" as he stared at my postpartum belly. I literally cried right there on the spot. If he only knew how much strength it took me to walk the length of the field in those shorts, he would have started clapping as I approached.

For over a decade, Brooks heard me correct people over and over again when they voiced how disappointed they thought he must be about us having ANOTHER sister. I'm thankful he wasn't scarred for life over the comments! I typically responded on his behalf with, "He's such a good brother to his sisters; he is excited to have another one." Or, "he's excited to have a say in who his future brothers-in-laws get to be one day." But as he got older, he started responding on his own with something like, "Honestly, I've gotten pretty good at handling sisters over the years so it's going to be welcomed, familiar territory."

On one such occasion, the reality set in on how many times comments were made with my children in tow.

An older gentleman quite literally yelled his judgment over the size of our family to the entire store with a comment we frequently heard, "Wow, you've got your hands full!" This particular time, Brooks responded with something I had said countless times before that made my heart skip a beat. He looked the elderly gentleman square in the eyes and matter-of-factly replied, "Sure does. Full of love." And that was the truth. My hands are more full of love than I ever imagined possible. Every time I used that response in the past, I meant it. But, the meaning didn't hit home until my own son repeated it back. I want my kids to see themselves as a blessing and a positive addition to my life. My life would not be as full of love, laughter, empathy, joy, significance, or emotion without each and every one of them.

It helps prepare in your mind what you want your responses to be when those situations arise. I've been known to correct people for their comments, but what good does that do? Why lecture when you can show your heart? If the comment hurts your feelings or exposes a raw nerve, take a moment and pray. Talk it over with the Lord. Ask Him what He wants you to see at that moment. I've found it is ok to be vulnerable with strangers. If they comment on your size, maybe share that as uncomfortable as you are, you are trying to keep the perspective that it is a blessing to sacrifice your comfort for your growing baby. For comments on the size of your family, perhaps share that you are "working on filling your quiver," which comes from Psalm 127:5, "Happy is the man that hath his quiver full of them." When you say the word quiver, it will either confuse those not familiar with that Bible verse, and they will leave pondering your amazing vocabulary, or it will tip off those familiar with the verse that you are a Christian. On many occasions this comment caused ladies to stop in their tracks and pray for our family, which is always such a treat.

The bottom line is people have a hard time avoiding the elephant in the room. Unfortunately the elephant is sometimes you. They genuinely want to brighten your day and make you laugh, but our emotions can get the best of us and pull us down into the trap of offense. And the older they are, the more I've found they really just want to start a conversation to get a window into reliving one of their memories they had with their own children with you. We stand to gain a lot of wisdom from those who have lived life experiences before us. Perhaps the conversation will bless your heart for years to come.

Before leaving this topic, one overarching feeling from people's comments must be addressed. For every scary, "life as you know it will never be the same," comment that is made, I want to pose that there is an equally beautiful, "life as you know it is just beginning," reality headed your way. When people talk about the lack of sleep and waking up in the middle of the night, they fail to mention there will be times your precious bundle is sleeping and you are eagerly waiting for them to wake up. You peek your eyes at them like a kid who can't keep their eyes off a big present holding their name under the Christmas tree. The baby starts stirring and at some points you may think, Oh, she will go back to sleep, but there will be times when the same stirring excites you into thinking, finally!! because you get to wake up the baby and be the first one to meet her eyes.

This, "finally she's awake!" excitement is how I picture Jesus when we wake up every single day; clapping, can't sit still in His seat. I imagine He's thinking, "I can't wait to spend time with her. What will we get to talk about and experience together today?!" So, as you embark on your journey through daily life, I encourage you to take Jesus' excitement over your encounters with others with you. He promises to never leave you. He patiently waits for your next prayerful thought to help guide the tone of your interactions today.

➡ **Jump to pages 166-170 in the Full Hands, Full Life Activity Companion Guide for this week's interactive prompts.**

Week 29: Documenting God Winks

Do you remember the required directional mapping to safely maneuver through stores during the Covid epidemic? What about the six feet apart X's at the checkout line? Perhaps those weren't the norm in your city, but in our hometown, there were taped arrows which mandated the permissible path through a store.

Funnily enough, there was an already established, unspoken path at one particular grocery store in town pre-Covid. You know, the kind of store where if you are a first-timer, you don't know the culture. One particular grocery store chain in our town frequently has a shopper standing out front asking to borrow a quarter, not knowing in advance the need for a quarter to untether their shopping cart from the others. In the aisles, an unsuspecting person clogs up the flow of shopping because everyone is swimming upstream two shopping carts wide, and they start trying to pass down the middle. Once you finish selecting your produce by the front entrance, the timer is on to check out and get your groceries home because the meat and fresh raspberries will start turning fast! Should you find yourself in the check out line, and heaven forbid forget something, you might as well check out and circle all the way back through the store and do it all again! The cashiers move those lines through faster than an untied balloon loses air. In fact, if you are paying with a card, it is expected you've already swiped it so the cashier only pushes the "pay now" button simultaneously as the last item is scanned. As the receipt is printed, you should be moving your new shopping cart away to start the self-bagging process so the cashier has space to pull your previous, now empty cart up to the end of the conveyor belt without delay. Although the experience can indeed be stressful, the price justifies the inconveniences of the shopping culture.

Well, Covid did not make the navigation arrows a new norm for this store; it just exacerbated the need for planning your trip through the store, making your list, and checking it twice. At the end of one particular trip with my son and three youngest daughters, we decided to use the new self checkout station. Bless all those fellow mommas who decide self checkout will be a fun experience for their kiddos. Extra blessing on those who resist the urge to take over the bagging as bread gets squished by half gallons of milk. Give those momma heroes a "we've all been there" smile next time you see one.

During this trip, my four year old got her inaugural chance at scanning. In her excitement at being mature enough for the most intricate role, she developed a bad habit of scanning the item over the reader and then in sheer elation of the beep happening whipped back around to smile and say "Got this one!" causing a duplicate scan. With a family of 8, we generally buy things in multiples so it would be ok as we would simply move the duplicate already existing in our buggy into the "bagging section.'" However, we had already scanned the "duplicate" item my precious daughter was holding. Since it was a mere $.89 can of black beans, a product which my family eats on the regular, I decided we could get a third and call it a day. No need to bother the cashier who already found herself in her rhythm of rapid scanning and dumping items for other customers–again remember the cadence with which she turns and burns groceries into carts with payments half way through processing. I turned to my capable son to ask him to please walk through–yes, BACKTRACK through the store–to get one more can of black beans. Now, I honestly did not know if he knew where said brand of black beans would be found. He was not a grocery store frequenter with me at this point in time as he typically elected to stay home with siblings who were napping to play video games or watch a sporting event as babysitting "payment." I felt like I was throwing him to the wolves. The line for self-checkout was steadily growing while judgmental eyes of bystanders questioned the viability of us claiming victory given our still-heaping buggy of groceries. As we were finishing up the final items my son rounded the corner, coming into view with the exact can of black beans in hand like a trophy. No sooner did he pass it to me, my eyes grazed the shelving unit next to the register to find, out of the tens of thousands of items in the store, the one item which was out of place and within arms length of checking out for me was a single can of the brand of black beans I had just sent my son to retrieve. I chuckled, pointed it out to my son, and said, "The Lord is so good, but also has such a sense of humor. Had I just looked two feet this direction, I would have seen that He knew this was going to happen and had some earlier, oblivious shopper previously place the exact item we needed here."

Many times the Lord's plan and answers for our questions are within reach, but without an aware eye, or when lacking time and space to gaze around, we can miss these little God-wink moments. I've found it incredibly valuable in my faith journey to document God-winks–those undeniable situations or events that occur in which you may say "that was lucky." In our house, we don't classify things as lucky. My husband started this years ago, and it has stuck through to today. Luck is just a time you get to see the Lord's hand undeniably moving in your life. Missing a car accident by seconds. Getting a new job against all odds. Having a hefty bill zeroed out before having to pay.

Receiving a surprise meal from a friend when looking into bare cupboards. I have a God-wink journal that I've carried around for years so I can reflect on moments the Lord was intentional to show me how seen and loved I am.

In Jeremiah 19, the Lord declares, "'For I know the plans I have for you,' says the LORD. 'They are plans for good and not for disaster, to give you a future and a hope.'" (Jeremiah 29:11, NLT).

What a promise from the Lord! If the Lord promises to prosper me, not harm me, give me hope and a future, I want to stay expectant and ready for those God-wink moments. I don't want to miss jotting down a single one, small or big. I've found that recognizing or noticing these moments gets easier. For some, it may be easier for you to spot these blessings in the lives of others. I encourage you to write them down and include the date. Many times these God-wink moments can feel like a rush of thankfulness or adrenaline. Other times they are tears of sheer joy, sometimes accompanied by feelings of unworthiness. When you jot down these mountain top experiences, it is easier to read back over them and keep your faith while walking through one of life's low points. The same Lord who provided for you on the mountaintop is still walking with you and providing for you in the valley. Take heart! He has overcome the world and all the valleys in it.

➡ Jump to pages 172-176 in the Full Hands, Full Life Activity Companion Guide for this week's interactive prompts.

Week 30: Beholding Nature's Beauty

As we round out the third quarter of our experiential journey together, we are closing out the section focused on relationships with others. This section has felt heavy but needed as we all experience relationships day in and day out. Sometimes those relationships are draining, even the good ones. Can I get an "Amen?"

Perspective shifts help me when I'm relationally drained out. As part of my role as a ministry leader, I'm tasked with taking a half day of solitude each month—four solid hours to spend time alone with my Creator and my thoughts. Usually when I share that part of my job description with people, I get one of two responses. "That sounds incredible! Sign me up!" or "That sounds terrible! I'd never be able to make it four hours alone without my (insert interruptions or devices of choice)."

For me, I've found this time most mentally cleansing and full of the Lord's presence when I get out in nature. It's not lost on me that from my vantage point where I write today, a hummingbird hovered by my window—no feeder or flowers in sight. I've never seen one here before, and the moment I looked up from my screen, a green hummingbird joined my writing journey on the precise day I'm writing about Beholding Nature's Beauty. You know what I say about coincidences . . . they are God-winks worth mentioning, so I wanted to jot this one down. It is not lost on me that the Lord directed the smallest known species of bird right in front of my window with wings fluttering 100-200 times per second, encouraging me to hover on this topic. Although the little bird hovered just a short while, I'm thankful for the moment our worlds collided and the encouragement its presence brought me.

I've spent many hours in solitude, hiking trails around our city. Within twenty-five miles of our home, in the suburbs of North Carolina, there are over fifteen unique hiking trails. On one particular hike, I remember feeling so overwhelmed with the thoughts of our children getting older. We had been able to replicate the baby ages six times over and felt we had a good grasp on those formative years, but the implications society was telling me about entering into teenage years overwhelmed me. Our kids were on the cusp of everything mattering, yet nothing important mattered to them. For the first time, grades were attached to transcripts, yet society said the normal teenager no longer cared about good grades. Society also boasts a teenager's inability to hear parental advice when they arguably need it the most. Their imminent futures place choices in front of them that hold compounding rewards and consequences.

How were we going to help them navigate demands of society and peer pressure? How could we create a strategy for success on healthy cell phone use? How would our kids respond to not having social media until they are eighteen? How can I help my daughters keep healthy self-images when the world constantly displays photoshopped and now AI-generated perfection?

While my mind swirled in this conversation with the Lord, I slowly approached a deep, wide culvert. My questions shifted to, *Lord, there has to be a way around this. There is no way people go down into the depths of that culvert without a path.* I looked around, but the path seemed to fall off the cliff before me. I kept traversing the path ahead. He whispered back, "the steps are all there. You've never been here, but I've been here many times before." How kind. How thoughtful. In the midst of my doubt on my proverbial path in life, where I felt completely unprepared for the motherhood road ahead, the Lord prepared a divine appointment for me to see His goodness and His grace first hand. Sure enough, the culvert held perfectly spaced out roots from the surrounding trees for footholds down and back up the other side. It was a magnificent sight to behold. Stairs would have washed away, but the roots dug in deep on both sides creating structure and stability only known by the Creator himself.

My conversation with the Lord instantly changed. *Thank you, Lord, for reminding me that while I am moving forward in this motherhood journey without all the answers, lacking confidence in many tough conversations, worried to share too much or too little of my story, I've got you, the only guide I need by my side. Let me listen to Your promptings. Let me trust that You love these kids more than I ever could. You have a plan for their lives to prosper them and not harm them. You want what is good for them and know what is best for them. Help me steer them in that direction for your plan is always perfect.*

Taking four hours to walk and talk in nature with the Lord fills my bucket back up. There is wisdom in what the Psalmist wrote:

When I consider your heavens, the work of your fingers, the moon and the stars, which you have set in place, what is mankind that you are mindful of them, human beings that you care for them?
Psalm 8:3-4

When we get out of our homes and step into the world all around us, we can begin to see how much the Lord delights in creating beauty for us to explore. When you start counting stars, or feel the breeze blowing yet can't see where it starts or ends, you gain perspective. When you stand at the top of a mountain and gaze over hundreds of thousands of trees in the valley below, you realize how small you are in comparison. Jesus himself attested to how valuable each and every one of us are in His father's eyes:

"Are not five sparrows sold for two pennies? Yet not one of them is forgotten by God. Indeed, the very hairs of your head are all numbered. Don't be afraid; you are worth more than many sparrows."
Luke 12:6-7

Of all the beautiful landscapes, river beds, crystal coasts, rainforest canopies, and snow covered mountaintops, God claims we are His majesty on display. Each person that ever has and ever will walk the face of this Earth somehow all bears the image of our Creator. Yet we are vastly different from one another. Why are we surprised? The Lord's delight in uniqueness is on display throughout the world. Although snowflakes are all the same on an atomic level, being made from hydrogen and oxygen atoms, it is impossible for two snowflakes to form complicated designs in exactly the same way. Each zebra's stripe pattern is unique from one another. Even twins, classified as identical from DNA level testing, hold their own uniquenesses. Two of my friends who have twins can attest to this phenomenon:

One commented on slight differentiations at birth, "Even though the girls were identical, right away we noticed one had hair that was a little darker, her skin tone was redder, and she had a more oval-shaped face. Her twin sister had lighter hair, a yellower skin tone and a round face with the sweetest little ears that stuck out just a bit."

The other shared the evolution of her daughter's uniqueness through the formative years, "The girls' distinct personalities and characteristics have been evident since they were born. One likes things to be more structured and routine-oriented, thriving on schedules and showing a strong desire not to miss out on anything. The other is more flexible, easygoing, and adaptable, sleeping longer and managing better even without strict routines. Their personalities also have become apparent in their roles at school; one likes to take on leadership and teacher-like roles, while the other prefers to be a supportive helper. All of this has amazed me at how God creates all of us differently with unique qualities and special gifts. It's so interesting to be able to see the special unique differences in our girls with them looking identical."

Chris and I both agree that seeing the beauty of the Lord's handiwork in all its vastness makes the undeniable case of a Creator setting the world in motion, so we seek ways to showcase that beauty to our children firsthand.

If you feel that you are stuck in a rut, tired of working diligently to find your people, set up boundaries, and release grudges, all while managing family dynamics, I suggest a mental escape outside. Get a change of scenery. Look for something that delights your heart outside of your own home. Something you did nothing to earn or grow, yet the Lord put its growth in motion so you could enjoy it at that very moment. My inclination tells me He will show up through nature more quickly than you believe possible.

➡️ **Jump to pages 178-182 in the Full Hands, Full Life Activity Companion Guide for this week's interactive prompts.**

Full Hands, Full Life

Weeks 31-40
Mothering Practicalities

Full Hands, Full Life

Week 31: Baby Elephant Syndrome

Welcome to the final quarter of our experiential devotional together. We turn our focus this quarter to strategies which help capitalize on this beautiful opportunity in our role as mothers.

What better way to jump in than by learning from one of the strongest mommas on planet Earth. The African bush elephant is capable of lifting 6,000kg, or about 13,225 lbs, from the lying down position. Even their trunks can lift over 200kg, thanks to containing over 40,000 muscles alone. For context, adult humans have just over 600 muscles in their entire bodies. Unlike humans, elephant calves come out of the womb (after 22 months gestation) weighing 200 - 300 pounds. Within 20 minutes of being born, calves can stand and begin walking within one hour. After just two short days, the infants can keep up with the herd. Strength is arguably the most essential defense characteristic for these large beasts, but the calf needs its mother for survival. They exclusively nurse for four months and then continue nursing three years after weaning to solid foods.

Harnessing the strength of these powerful beasts

became a quest for native people groups in both Africa and Asia, yet domesticating these animals is no small feat. Elephant handlers only realize success when the process starts from infancy. As soon as the baby can be weaned from its mother, it is tied to a tree. At first, the babies try to resist and break free. They refuse to eat and drink for nearly eight days while they muster all their focus on breaking the rope or chain wrapped around their leg. After only a few short weeks, a mental paradigm shift occurs. The baby elephant grows up becoming strong enough to break free yet won't try. It remains trapped inside a mental cage more fortified than the original chain itself.

From this animal taming practice, the term "Baby Elephant Syndrome" entered the world of therapy in 1967 by psychotherapist George Weinberg. According to Segen's Medical Dictionary, this is a "hopeless helplessness learned in childhood, which becomes hard-wired in a person's psyche as he or she develops and matures."[23]

When I first learned of this concept, I began reflecting back on my childhood. What things were spoken over me that tethered me down? Were there circumstances I experienced that became shackled chains? One recurring theme surfaced—my musical talent only reached as far as the piano. In middle school, I accompanied our choir for concerts. However, deep down, I wanted to sing, and more importantly, I wanted a solo. I auditioned. I perfectly sang the solo—pitches, articulation, and rhythms. Then I distinctly remember my choir director chuckling, "Now I see why you make such a great accompanist. Your voice is precise, not free like a soloist." My dreams were shattered. I never tried out for a solo again.

My musical interest continued through college where I studied music education, but also minored in Spanish as a second, future option. Upon entering junior year, a required vocal audition hung over the heads of all the vocal music students. Three choir placements existed for me: the non-audition Women's Choir, the large audition group—University Chorale, and the elite, hand selected

Chamber Singers. This last group was a pipe dream of all choral education majors as the number of auditioned vocalists far exceeded the capped number of spots that became available each year. A student's best chance at being selected for Chamber Singers came during their senior year or their master's program.

I remember joking with my friend, Jessica, who happens to be a traveling, high soprano opera singer delighting crowds worldwide, how unfair it was that my audition bumped right up next to hers. Even as a junior, she was a shoo-in with Chamber Singers in my opinion, yet she approached the audition with reverence.

Rosters for the choirs were posted after a few days. Jessica, always a bundle of energy, dragged me up the spiral staircase to the second floor of the school of music and ran to the taped papers which hung our fate. With the rosters alphabetized, she found her name nearly at the top of the Chamber Singers list and silently screamed, jumping up and down in the hall.

Jessica began reading out who else was in Chamber Singers with her. Suddenly she stopped reading and wide-eyed with a full, open-mouth smile turned to me and said my name.

My first reaction was that there must be some mistake. Chamber Singers as a junior?

When I saw our choir conductor, I shared my feelings of disbelief. His response echoed my middle school choir director's comments, but it landed in such a different way. He commented that my knack for sight reading and blendable, choir voice would ground the intonation of the second soprano section for years.

Chains broken.

In what ways are you experiencing 'baby elephant syndrome' in your own life? How about in your mothering journey? Dr. Belynder Walia, in her article titled "5 Tell-Tale Signs You Are Suffering From Baby Elephant Syndrome" eloquently writes, "The syndrome occurs when we hold onto bad feelings and emotions for so long that they become part of our identity. We start to identify with them so much that we think they're who we are instead of just something we sometimes feel."[24]

I became the girl who could sing, but preferred to play piano. Had the chains been tight enough, the middle school solo offense too heavy to bear, I may have given up on choir altogether—or perhaps even music as a whole—stifling the life I now know from coming to fruition. During a Chamber Singers performance, Chris saw me on stage and gained the courage to ask me out to lunch. The rest, as they say, is history.

Our love of music formed the starting point of our relationship, and we've shared this love of music with our own children. All are singers. All play a variety of instruments. Several enjoy the theatrical stage, and so far, they all began playing or singing in the youth worship band at church when they reached middle school age. Watching their God-given abilities grow into ways to serve the Lord, ushering peers into a posture of worship, brings tears to my eyes.

Like elephants, humans often never forget. When we are upset about something—an insult, a break up, a disagreement, a failed attempt, a pattern of safety or food insecurity—we hold on to it, like the proverbial elephant on our back. But, we weren't intended to hold that kind of weight. Those moments fester and change our outlook on ourselves and our abilities.

As mothers, we owe it to ourselves and our littles to reflect back on childhood. Most of us can pinpoint sayings, house rules, or circumstances we never want to repeat with our children. Sure, there are safety nets I want to place around my children to help them navigate life gracefully. But, I don't want to tether them in place, through my words or actions, in such a way that they lose sight of their God-given strengths and abilities. Instead of fearing them experiencing embarrassment or receiving a "you're not good enough" label, I help them memorize lines, take them to auditions, give them piano lessons, cheer the loudest from the audience, and keep reminding them that it is not the opinion of others that stems their self-worth; the never-changing thoughts and loving opinions their Heavenly Father holds of them creates the foundation of their life's value.

The Good News of the Gospel is that our God is more powerful than an entire herd of unchained elephants. In Acts 16, Paul and Silas, two famous apostles for Christ, after being severely flogged, thrown into the inner cell of a prison in stocks, start praying and singing hymns to God. The other prisoners were listening to them when, "Suddenly there was such a violent earthquake that the foundations of the prison were shaken. At once all the prison doors flew open, and everybody's chains came loose." (Acts 16:26) This incredible story concludes with Paul and Silas, telling the prison guard who was about to take his own life about how to believe in Jesus and save his whole family.

The same God who was in the business of breaking chains then, is still in the business of breaking through our chains now. When we seek Him through prayer and worship, He promises to respond by sending a needed earthquake to rattle our own prison doors and set our captive hearts free.

➡ Jump to pages 184-188 in the Full Hands, Full Life Activity Companion Guide for this week's interactive prompts.

Full Hands, Full Life

Week 32: Fragility of Infants

What is more humbling than the Lord Himself, the King of Kings, volunteering to come into the world in the most fragile of states—that of a newborn baby. The One who would bear the weight of the entire world on His shoulders had to learn to walk, talk, and crawl just like the rest of us. He fell just like our toddlers. He cried when He got bumps and bruises. Jesus Himself, needed His mother, Mary, to nurse Him, wipe His tears, and cuddle Him during His formative years.

Philippians 2 explains it this way, Jesus, "Who, being in very nature a God, did not consider equality with God something to be used to his own advantage; rather, he made himself nothing by taking the very nature b of a servant, being made in human likeness. And being found in appearance as a man, he humbled himself by becoming obedient to death—even death on a cross! (Philippians 2:6-8). He could have shown up in any form, yet He chose total dependence and took on the form of man.

The Lord calls us into a posture of total dependence on Him. Since Jesus is our guidepost on creating a relationship with the God of the universe, sending Him into the world in our identical, vulnerable state makes perfect sense. In His vulnerable, infant state, Jesus relied on Joseph and Mary's trust in God to keep Him safe.

As first time parents, they likely held the same feelings many of us share—feeling overwhelmed and unprepared, yet in awe of this tiny human given to our care.

When Leighton, our third child, was only three months old, we took her with us to a wedding in the mountains. Although the wedding was in the last month of winter, the weather cooperated beautifully. During the rehearsal dinner, the doors to the venue were flung open to let the sounds of the downtown atmosphere fill the space. We spent hours toasting the bride and groom, rehashing memories once forgotten about their younger years. Leighton was a perfect angel sleeping in her car seat nearly the entire time. Passersby gazed in delight at her sweet disposition as she dozed in her puffy pink dress, tiny navy cardigan, and darling matching bow.

After the rehearsal dinner, Chris and I headed back to the hotel. As I was changing Leighton into her footed pajamas, I noticed how hot her skin felt to the touch. Perhaps it was all the layers and being tucked away in the car seat for so long. Then I noticed her labored breathing. Her piercingly blue eyes were ghostly and void of any recognition. Being out of town, I didn't have a thermometer, but I knew something was wrong. I needed to bring her fever down fast. I jumped into a bath with her, submerging her body in the water that was cool to the touch. She didn't cry. My heart stopped. Babies always cry when you put them in tepid water. Especially babies whose body temperature is high with fever. Then, I saw her belly sinking and rising with every breath.

In these instances, your mind races a million miles a minute. *How can I fix my baby? What did I forget to do for her today? Was the weather too cold for her? Is the fever why she slept so well at the party? Is her coloring looking strange? Are her eyes rolling back?* Both of these last two questions became a quick yes while in the bath. She started looking jaundiced, and her eyes were sinking and losing focus. Then, her lips turned blue and her stomach stopped breathing. I screamed for Chris. Within 60 seconds flat, we frantically rushed through the hotel lobby hollering at the night time concierge to point us in the direction of the local hospital—Chris with the diaper bag and car seat in hand, me clutching our sweet, limp baby on my chest in a blanket.

If I knew what I know now, I would have slowed my own breathing and recited the promise, "The LORD himself goes before you and will be with you; he will never leave you nor forsake you. Do not be afraid; do not be discouraged" (Deuteronomy 31:8). In the car, I would have started giving thanks for the way the Lord promised to go before us and prepare clear roads and favorable waiting times in the ER. I would have asked Him to give us an ER doctor who specializes in infant care. But my relationship with the Lord has grown leaps and bounds over the last decade, so these were not the thoughts running through my head.

I remember watching her breathing stop again as I tried putting her in the car seat. Chris pulled up to a red light and I begged him to turn on the flashers and just go. I remember saying, "I'm losing her," as tears flooded the top of my shirt. We arrived at the emergency department and Chris jolted the car in park before the wheels stopped turning, and we rushed in searching for someone to help our baby.

Mary and Joseph, unwed teenagers from humble upbringings, exemplified listening to the promptings of their heavenly Father to protect Jesus time and time again. After the three wise men from the East had presented their gifts to baby Jesus, "...an angel of the Lord appeared to Joseph in a dream. 'Get up,' he said, 'take the child and his mother and escape to Egypt. Stay there until I tell you, for Herod is going to search for the child to kill him.' So he got up, took the child and his mother during the night and left for Egypt" (Matthew

2:13-14). This act of obedience, fleeing everything they had once known—family, friends, job security, the language—to bravely travel under the cover of darkness to a foreign country, kept King Herod from finding and killing Jesus. It took Mary and Joseph years of personal sacrifice to keep baby Jesus safe.

In our case, we weren't fleeing for safety; we were searching for restored health. We knew Leighton was sick beyond our parenting experience. We needed a rescue. Her three month old body was pricked and prodded; she was hooked up to monitors and IVs and lay limp in my arms in the emergency room bed. After three days in the hospital and passing a car seat safety test, the Lord answered our prayers with Leighton battling through pneumonia and being allowed to return home. The three hour ride back towards our two littles still at home was nerve-wracking to say the least. We had to monitor and count her breaths every couple of minutes. A sleeping baby in a car seat tends to slump their neck down just enough to make it more laborious to breathe, especially ones with compromised lung capacity. We documented each exit that housed a hospital along our route to know which direction to head should her oxygen levels become depleted. The miracle of this situation continued to unfold over the next several years, both in terms of continued health for Leighton and financial relief from the unexpected hospital stay. Had we not been in tune with caring for our sweet Leighton and left her in the car seat to sleep overnight, this story may have ended in a tragedy.

Since Jesus willingly entered the world in the dependent, infant state, He understands how we enter into relationships with the same dependence. We don't ask our babies to start doing chores and earn their keep. We feed them, clothe them, and clean them, all while asking nothing in return. It is only as they develop and earn their trust that we start inviting them into more responsibilities.

In His short three years in ministry, Jesus exemplified so many nurturing roles to His disciples that we as mothers are invited to showcase to our children. With a humble, loving spirit, Jesus listened to, provided for, advocated for, cheered on, prayed for, prayed with, guided, led, corrected, taught, protected, believed, encouraged, held, included, spent time with, danced with, laughed with, and cried with his disciples. The disciples asked questions of Jesus over and over again. Jesus explained the same topics repeatedly knowing full well they would not fully grasp their meaning until later in life. Does all this sound familiar? If Jesus's example of relationship with the fragile, dependent disciples He called into ministry is one to emulate, we should approach the role of mother with the same heart posture of Jesus. Jesus knew the future ahead for His disciples and interacted with them day in and day out with that perspective in mind.

What would it look like for us to not take these "here and now" nurturing roles for granted? Would we choose to slow down and hold our kids longer, dance with them in the kitchen while the dishes wait, join them as they watch an episode of their favorite show without our devices in hand able to engage in conversations on character interactions? Would we include them more in our day-to-day activities instead of coveting the ability to grocery shop or run errands alone? Only through emulation of Jesus' ability to be wholly present and fully engaged with His disciples will I shepherd my kids into the full life each day affords. Perhaps you, like I, would need a supernatural blessing of energy and patience renewed every single day to make this remotely possible. Thankfully we serve a God who delights in restoring grace, patience, and mercy with the dawn of each new day.

There is beauty in fragility. There is dependency in fragility. Let us approach that aspect of our role as mothers in the same way Jesus did with His disciples - with utmost respect and responsibility.

**➡️ Jump to pages 190-194 in the
Full Hands, Full Life Activity Companion Guide
for this week's interactive prompts.**

Week 33: Phases of Life

Can we start this week by sending up a quick praise to the Lord for making babies enter the world stationary? Did he know us, or did he know us?! Imagine just for a second how different the launch into motherhood would be if our children came out running. For the adoptive mothers who did not experience the newborn pace into motherhood, I am in awe of each of you. In my fifteen years of experience in child rearing, I've found that just about the time I'm ready for a kid to be in the next phase of life, they arrive in it. I couldn't imagine it any other way.

In our home, we affectionately refer to the phases of life growth spurts by these benchmarks:

* *Holding hands comfortably height*: Walking next to the baby gets so comfy without slouching that their hand slips right out from yours as they stumble.

* *Tabletop height*: The first time they stand up under the table and you hear the "thump" of their head.

* *Doorknob height*: When they cut the corner too closely and knock their noggin on the doorknob.

* *Elbow height*: When they sneak up behind you in the kitchen and you elbow them in the forehead while pulling a drawer open (this has literally happened to each of my children!)

By using these uncomfortable moments as milestones to celebrate, their attention is quickly diverted from the pain they are experiencing to high fives around the room.

Aside from physical growth markers for the phases of life, I find our intellectual and spiritual growth mirror the development of the art of bartering to get what we want. Infants cry. Toddlers throw temper tantrums. Kids sometimes run away upset, hiding until someone comes to find them. Pre-teens often act out. By high school, children start being willing to give up certain treasured rights if it means they get what they value more. The growth through phases of life in bartering ultimately grows into adulthood when larger financial decisions require bartering of sorts.

Anyone who has walked on a car lot understands the expectation for bartering. One time I went to just look at cars and told my husband I did not need him to come with me because I was either driving home in the car I rode in on or one off the lot. We had just had our third baby and all were in car seats. Brooks was in a tall booster, Ellie was in a transitional five point harness, and Leighton was in the rear facing infant seat. To venture out around town, I secured them all in their car seats and instructed Brooks and Ellie to raise their hands while I slammed the door closed. If their hands weren't raised, they ran the risk of car seats colliding and fingers getting pinched. We packed them in like sardines! The issue was, we knew the kids were only getting bigger, and they didn't fit in the back seat as it was already.

Long story short, I drove away that day with the showroom model of a new, larger car but had made a profit on the car I traded in. They paid us enough to not only pay off what we still owed on my trade-in, but also the full down payment and the first couple months of our new car. All this was because I was willing to drive away in my current car while I waited for them to offer all the bells and whistles of the extended maintenance plan with service visits included for the first three years. I bartered from a vantage point of knowing the threshold of what I wasn't willing to sacrifice just for the sake of getting a new car.

So, where are you on the bartering scale of life? Are you temper-tantrum throwing, or are you masterfully wheeling and dealing? What about your motherhood journey? 2 Timothy 2:22 urges us to, "Flee the evil desires of youth, and pursue righteousness, faith, love, and peace, along with those who call on the Lord out of a pure heart."

Having a baby catapults you into adulthood in a way nothing else does. The desires of your youth may still be present, but the infant in your care puts things into perspective instantaneously. However, simply having a baby does not make all the fleshly desires of our youth disappear. Life would be so much easier if that was the case!

Youthful desires span topics beyond the top three most common offenders: sex, drugs, and alcohol. Popularity, gossiping, status, beauty, money, coveting, and jealousy just skim the surface of the youthful desires list. The verse from 2 Timothy tells us we must flee these desires. The definition of flee is to run away from a place or situation of danger. We are supposed to run the opposite direction from our youthful, or immature desires, understanding that they are a danger to our ability to move forward into the next phase of life the Lord has in store for us. Using our adult skill of bartering, we gain momentum in discerning the give and take between what our fleshly desires scream for and the misalignment of those desires with the full life of our future. We are to run, full steam ahead, towards righteousness, faith, love and peace. If we aren't running towards those things, how can we shepherd our children in that direction?

I find encouragement in the preposition the next phase of the verse holds: with. We are to flee these evil desires along with those who call on the Lord out of a pure heart. Did you catch that seemingly small detail? We will not be the only ones fleeing these evil desires. There will be others fleeing in the same direction who we can run with! Who are these people we are to run with? Those who call on the Lord out of a pure heart. These individuals have the same motivation you and I have—pursuing righteousness, faith, love, and peace. Don't those people sound like the kind of folks you want to be around? Equally as important, don't they sound like the kind of people you want your children to have as mentors in their life?

As we established in Week 21, we are stronger together. God did not intend us to live life on our own. He created us for community. One aspect of a strong community working towards a common goal is accountability. Accountability is vitally important; we can easily deceive ourselves into believing that we can hide in the darkness, but when light shines on the darkness it makes the darkness flee (John 1:5). Sometimes it is someone in our community who offers their spark to help light our own candle. Sometimes it is someone fleeing darkness who brings batteries for your flashlight. But sometimes it is someone who will walk into your dark space and bring their own lantern, willing to stay with you until daylight comes.

In motherhood, we experience times when we need help bringing light into our dark spaces of fleshly desires. Through continual personal growth and authentic relationships our light is restored. From there, with our lanterns fully lit, we gain perspective to help our children grow through the phases of life, providing the light for them to barter through decisions while fleeing the evil desires of their hearts.

➡️ **Jump to pages 196-200 in the Full Hands, Full Life Activity Companion Guide for this week's interactive prompts.**

Week 34: Fear Removal

Chris and I prioritize traveling and experiencing adventure with our kids, even if it stretches our own preferred adventure levels. Traveling with kids, regardless of the number, adds complexity to the logistics, but traveling with six children adds exponential costs and liability in all situations. Whether it is a day excursion in our local town or one multiple states away, we want to create time and space of wonder for our kids to contemplate the divine Creator of our universe.

Several years ago, we started taking our musically inclined kids to concerts. We began at our local church and quickly advanced to other venues in neighboring cities. When one of our favorite worship bands posted the first leg of their upcoming tour was heading to Nashville, we thought through the logistics. Being the closest city on the tour, Nashville was a seven-hour road trip from home, but still doable with just one overnight stay in a hotel (a luxury our kids seldom experience). The trip there was picturesque. When we left the house at 4am, I have to admit my grouchiness over Chris's request to leave at the ungodly time in the middle of the night put a dark cloud over the vibe in the car. The idea that the kids would fall back asleep in the car for a few hours was a pipe dream. Never having traveled to Nashville nor seen an arena filled for the purpose of worship, none of them got any shuteye along the way. My attitude completely shifted as Chris's timing had us meeting the North Carolina mountain roads just in time to watch the last of the stars leave the sky while the sun peeked over the horizon of the mountaintops. The sky filled with hundreds of colorful hues resembling a full sky rainbow, which delighted the youngest among us.

Psalm 19:1 came to mind, "The heavens declare the glory of God, and the sky above proclaims his handiwork" (ESV). The same God who controls the rising and setting of the sun, who paints the sky with these majestic colors day and day out, is the same God who loves me from everlasting to everlasting. We chatted about this in the car and the purpose of the trip was in full swing.

The concert was epic. Our son, a new drummer at the time, got a perfect view of the drummer from our seats. Our girls, who naturally love singing harmonies together, got to witness live worship on a large scale, widening their dreams of using their God-given vocal talents for the Lord. The scale of production was beyond impressive, and the close proximity of Nashville's Bridgestone Arena to the downtown food hall let us organically meet married musicians, Kari Jobe & Cody Carnes, on their way to dinner. We took a picture which undeniably captured my growing baby bump, so we posted it on social media as Lila's pregnancy reveal. All moments we will cherish forever.

But, traveling back to NC, the weather turned nasty. We elected to take the pathway north, through Kentucky to avoid the NC mountain highways. As the large rain storm rolled through Kentucky, our van suddenly broke down. Chris wrestled it to the side of the road while every warning light flashed and alarms sounded from the dash. Our trip came to an abrupt halt. When the tow truck arrived, he didn't have room for our entire family but recognized stranding us on the side of the highway in a rainstorm seemed like an impractical solution. So instead, he instructed us to lay all of our seats back as far as they could, jacked our car up on the tow truck, and pulled us a few miles to the nearest convenience store.

During this time, our kids watched our every move. They fed off our emotions. Instead of voicing my concern over getting illegally towed while still inside the vehicle, I praised the tower's willingness to weigh all the circumstances and choose the least dangerous option. Instead of voicing the uneasy feeling I got as the tow truck pulled away, stranding our family at the dirty mom & pop convenience store with no other establishment in sight, we chose to remain calm and weigh out our options. After the dealership in this small town finally located a vehicle large enough to transport us all together, I started putting together how late we would be arriving home. Given the late arrival, our childcare solution for Lydia, who was two at the time and stayed at home, was coming to an end. We were over four hours away from home with no transportation option in sight. Anxiety crept in. Chris saw the fear in my eyes and pulled me aside to make a quick plan together. Chris and I started making calls, lining up care for Lydia through the night. Family back home jumped in to help, but we were still stuck entertaining four kids in a dealership in Kentucky for an undisclosed amount of time. We made the most of it letting the kids enjoy the popcorn, ice cream sandwiches, and water available in the service department. We made games using the furniture and visited every area of the dealership accessible to clients. While entertained, fear of the unknown couldn't creep into the hearts of our kids. Eventually the service technicians admitted not finding the cause of the car breaking down and sent us home in a rental for further investigation.

When the kids retell this story, they talk about the adventure—how wild it was seeing the sky instead of the road when we were being towed, how unlimited popcorn really can make your tummy ache, how fun it was to drive a new car around for a couple weeks. Our attitudes and experiences in life form their own perception of events.

This rings true in the normal routines as well. If you hold a fear of heights, roller coasters, elevators, animals, water, spiders, snakes, storms, close spaces, dentists, crowds, public speaking, or any of the other top fears in the world, it is likely your fear will be projected onto your child. By overcoming your fears, you set an example of taming fear. Prevailing over and overcoming fears in your life is obtainable through the work of the Holy Spirit. For the sake of your children, it may be necessary. If we want to grow courageous, strong, and capable adults, then we want to avoid creating any unnecessary fears in their lives at all costs.

Sometimes fears creep in as children observe those fears expressed in others around them. I remember the first time Brooks witnessed a friend scared by storms. He happened to be at his friend's house in the midst of a summer thunderstorm. The next time thunder started rumbling through the sky at home, he reacted in a way I had never seen from him before. We talked through it together and we made a game of counting the time between thunder and lightning. I remember my own dad teaching me how to track the proximity of storms in this manner, "One Mississippi, two Mississippi, three Mississippi. Oh! It's now three miles away." Throughout my growing up years, Dad could sense my fear growing when facing the unknown. Instead of a quick dismissal of my feelings, he took the longer route of educating me beyond my worry. Dad knows how to fix just about everything. His keen eye picks up on appliances wearing down, vehicles needing maintenance, and feasible repair options instead of costly replacements.

To this day his week never gets too busy to send quick reminder texts to disconnect our hoses with the forecasts' upcoming freeze warnings, or check my oil reading in my car. Yet with his sixth sense for evaluating the status of the "machines" of this world, he also possesses the keen awareness of the feelings of others. As a child, he picked up how sharing his vast knowledge translated into the growth of my courage. So just like I did with dad, in the midst of the storm, Brooks and I talked about how the Lord made the sound of thunder help you track whether the storm was coming or going. Now when we see bolts of lightning light up the sky like fireworks on the 4th of July, we marvel at the Lord's light show on display.

In one particularly long hurricane, whose outer rings hovered over our area for several days, we experienced torrential rain causing widespread flooding and power outages. The kids and I noticed water pouring down the street in front of our house towards the storm drain. We put on bathing suits, rain jackets, and headed out front with pool inner tubes in tow. They spent hours "white water rafting" down the street in front of our house. Now every time we have a rain storm roll through without thunder and lightning, they head outside to raft down the street.

Another very tangible way to combat fear is through educating proper reactions to fearful situations. Children drowning in a body of water is a warranted fear. Precautions need to be made to minimize chances for this horrific accident to occur. During one trip to our friends' neighborhood pool, I lost track of Leighton, who was three at the time. She was playing in the shallow end one moment and the next thing I knew, she had walked down the steps directly into the four foot section. Normally this would not be a problem as she would have her floaties on, but this particular time she had taken them off. The scary thing about children drowning is that their bodies go into self preservation mode. Instead of using energy and oxygen to flail around and scream out, they freeze, conserving oxygen for keeping the internal organs functioning to stay alive. So, when I saw her, she was completely motionless standing on the bottom of the pool, with only her crystal blue eyes wide open staring in my direction—a haunting, helpless look of distress. I've never moved so fast at eight months pregnant in my life. I jumped in the water and scooped her up in one sweeping motion. My confidence in taking my three young children to this pool was that lifeguards were always on duty; however, this time, the rope of the lifeguard's red rescue tube got tangled around the arms of his chair preventing him from being able to dive in. In the time he struggled to break free I already had her poolside coughing the water from her lungs. This was a formative moment in Leighton's life. I could have gone off on the lifeguard, stormed away from the pool, and created a huge scene. Instead I wrapped her up in a towel, held her as close as my growing belly would allow, and calmed her down. I reassured the lifeguard that he would have gotten to her in time; I just happened to be closer. I told him how special it was for me to get to save her, but also apologized for not watching her closely enough to see the floaties were missing from her arms. Before we left the pool that day, Leighton understood the importance of the floaties and learning how to swim. She loves the water to this day but has a new respect for it.

Ultimately, when we approach life with the mindset of Psalm 46:1-3, fear gives way to peace in the face of our Father's power and protection.

"God is our refuge and strength, a very present help in trouble. Therefore we will not fear though the earth gives way, though the mountains be moved into the heart of the sea, though its waters roar and foam, though the mountains tremble at its swelling. Selah"
Psalm 46:1-3 (ESV)

Invite the Lord to be your confidence in times when fear grips hold of your heart. Ask Him to give you the proper level of fear to keep you safe but not the level that inhibits you or your child's ability to thrive in situations. I've seen lifelong fears disappear in my own life for the sake of my children. My prayer is that you will experience these same victories in your life from this day forward.

**➡ Jump to pages 202-206 in the
Full Hands, Full Life Activity Companion Guide
for this week's interactive prompts.**

Week 35: Natural Motherly Instincts / Postpartum

To date, you've known and sensed your child's presence longer than anyone else on Earth. How does that fact land with you? If we flip that statement, your child has known you longer than anyone else on Earth. Watching a newborn relax into their mom's chest as they hear the familiar pattern of her heartbeat and voice is a sight to behold.

For all of us, natural motherly instincts are involuntary at first. Your body does the work while the baby grows in utero. The internal shifts that happen while pregnant, like mood swings, nausea, exhaustion, weight gain, all point to this new life forming. As the baby starts moving, you get the reassuring butterfly kisses in your belly. No one else gets to feel the exact butterfly kiss from your child like you do.

Something happens when a new baby is born. Within days, hours, minutes, even seconds, imagining life before this little one seems impossible. You look into this itty, bitty baby's eyes and see a world of potential. The kicks and turns and inward hugs you've been experiencing all these months instantly have a face to go along with them—eyes that peer into your soul like a forever friend. The sound of your voice calms their cries and the warmth of your arms creates the safe space they long for after the cold, bright surroundings invaded their inner sanctuary.

Bonding with a newborn seems so natural. It seems innate and obvious. So what happens when the "natural" instincts don't kick in? With the birth of a newborn, a flood of emotions come rushing in—excitement, joy, and perhaps fear and anxiety. Struggling with unwanted emotions after childbirth is not a character flaw and happens more often than you think. Sometimes, these emotions are even a side effect of birth itself, but ignoring these red flags could be detrimental to your health and ability to care for your little one.

After the traumatic birth of my second child, which I wrote about in Week 16, I experienced mild postpartum depression symptoms now coined as the "baby blues." The Mayo Clinic's website explains, "most new moms experience postpartum 'baby blues' after childbirth, which commonly include mood swings, crying spells, anxiety and difficulty sleeping. Baby blues usually begin within the first 2 to 3 days after delivery and may last for up to two weeks."[25] Postpartum depression, reported to occur in 15% of women shortly before or after childbirth, presents like the baby blues, but symptoms are more intense and can last up to several months.[26]

If you feel your motherly instincts aren't going to kick in or didn't kick in, know that you are not alone. Dealing with postpartum depression or thoughts of inadequacy in motherhood is very real. Arguably the worst part about this prognosis is that you won't know if you will struggle with it until the struggling arrives, and many times those who are battling negative mindsets don't notice or admit it themselves. In these cases, allowing loved ones to point out symptoms, even when they are hard and painful to hear can be a lifeline towards recovery. Take the postpartum screenings at your well-baby visits. Even the most severe postpartum depression cases can be resolved quicker with early detection.

Mothering Practicalities

In hindsight, after having my second, I wish I had asked for more help from friends and family. Instead I hunkered down and tried to take care of her by myself, ignoring my recovery. I should have taken people up on the offer to come sit and hold her while I took a nap. I should have said yes to the offers to do laundry and play with our son, Brooks, so I could have more time to bond with Ellie. Yet, even in the midst of the baby blues, the natural instincts, the way the Lord intended for mothers and children to bond, began kicking in.

One instinct that baffles my mind is how quickly we pick up on our own child's cry. In a matter of hours, we go from never having heard it to being able to pick their cry out from a crowd. In fact, mothers can differentiate between the signaling cries of her newborn: I'm hungry, I'm tired, something hurts, change my britches! Only in proximity with one another can these cues be picked up on.

When our son was nine months old, Chris and I traveled to Boston for a wedding anniversary trip. Still nursing at the time, Brooks got to tag along with us. We enjoyed sightseeing around town, taking double decker tour buses to hop between famous landmarks while learning history of the historic city from tour guides along the way. We returned to the hotel one night completely exhausted. Given my germaphobe tendencies, I couldn't fathom putting Brooks in his pajamas before bathing the germs of the city away. So, I ran the bath water and plopped him in the tub. Being our first trip away from home with a baby in tow, I had packed nearly the entire house, including his bath toys. Unbeknownst to me, Brooks found the complimentary shampoo and conditioner resting on the corner of the tub. Also unbeknownst to me, Brooks was able to unscrew said tiny bottles of shampoo and conditioner. He did what any nine month old would do and promptly put the bottle top in his mouth. Realizing he had gotten quiet I turned around to find him wide eyed and still. Seeing the bottle of shampoo pouring out into the water, I instinctively knew the cap was in his throat. All the newborn CPR class literature took over.

I instinctively flipped him over with his belly on my forearm, and used the palm of my other hand in the middle of his back to dislodge the cap. Hearing Brooks start his "I'm hurt" cry, Chris rushed in, and I told him I'd never been more happy to hear a baby cry in my life. Crisis averted.

Much like learning our own childrens' voices, spending time in prayer and talking with Jesus grows our familiarity with our Savior's guiding voice in our life. In John 10, Jesus states, "My sheep listen to my voice; I know them, and they follow me" (v.27). This verse brings to mind a YouTube video I once saw of a Norwegian shepherd teaching tourists his sheep call. When a tourist tried, the sheep never moved. Yet, when the shepherd stepped out in a field of hundreds of sheep mixed together from surrounding farms, every single one of his sheep fell in line and came running to him as he called out. The most remarkable thing was that other sheep also stood in the field, and they continued grazing, unfazed. Jesus promises we can reach this familiarity in listening to His voice, the voice of our Good Shepherd.

We never know the precise moments when our motherly instincts will take over, but I like to thank God each time my senses are perked for His watchful eyes on my children. I listen for those promptings of the Holy Spirit to take a quick peek in the backyard to check in on the kids, send a text to one of my older kids asking how the time over at their friend's house is going, or sit in bed with one to ask what really happened at dance class that caused their long face all evening. God knows and sees our children in the same way He knows and sees us. Inviting Him into our relationship and parenting of them is an upgrade to instinctual motherly intuition I never want to pass up.

➡️ **Jump to pages 208-212 in the Full Hands, Full Life Activity Companion Guide for this week's interactive prompts.**

Week 36: Schedule Reliability

As people so graciously remind you, having a baby changes your life forever. Many times they are referring to all the horrible ways—lack of sleep, lack of routine, lack of ability to enjoy things you once did. However, by working towards a schedule in your children's lives, you get to invite them into healthy rhythms of sleep, work, and play. The outcome is getting to enjoy life with your children by your side.

One of the most beautiful rewards of sharing life with your children is getting to view even the mundane tasks in a childlike way. So often I'm simply driving them to afternoon activities and one of the littles highlights a funny shaped cloud in the sky or comments on the expression on the person's face next to us at a stoplight. These comments remind me to raise my perspective to a heavenly one, seeking His presence in our surroundings. They remind me that behind the eyes of every person in our path lies a story and a child bearing the image of Christ himself. We often pray for those with downcast expressions to have an unexpected blessing to cheer up their spirits, or when people around us drive with reckless abandon, we pray for the logistics of their day to allow for them to slow down and pause. When ambulances or fire trucks pass by, we pray for the first responders, those who may be suffering or in pain, and for the families of all those involved. These moments help center us all in the midst of our day.

Sleep is another area where structure and consistency is beneficial. As I mentioned in Week 3 of this journey together, Chris and I employed the use of the sleep training routine outlined in the book, On Becoming Babywise: Giving Your Infant the GIFT of Nighttime Sleep, by Robert Bucknam M.D. & Gary Ezzo. The routine establishes a healthy rhythm of eating, playing, and sleeping from infancy. Typically the thought process behind a baby sleeping for a long time is to fill the baby's tummy full so the calories keep them asleep as long as possible. The only problem with this process is that when the baby wakes up they feel terrible. Think about that uncomfortable feeling you wake up to after a post-Thanksgiving meal nap. You don't feel rested. You feel bloated and lethargic. Why would we expect our babies to feel any different? I remember a sing-song book I read to my kids before bedtime that had a line I still use to this day, "God made our bodies to need rest so when we wake up we feel our best." From the beginning, sleep became a reward, not a punishment in our home.

The Babywise routine encourages feeding the babies, then playing with them to keep them awake. When they get fussy, you know they either have a dirty diaper or they are tired. You check their diaper and change it if needed, or you know they are sleepy and lay them down for a nap. When they wake up, you know they are waking up because they are hungry and feed them. It naturally limits the stressful moments when your babies are crying, unable to communicate what is wrong with them, and you lack an answer to fix their discomfort. In addition to minimizing moments of frustration, most babies start sleeping six to eight hours uninterrupted by six weeks of age. And, even at that, you feed them once and put them down for another four hours. The only child of ours who struggled with sleeping long stretches at night was our little one who had an undetected milk allergy until after her second birthday. So, of course she had more tummy discomfort as dairy existed in my diet while breastfeeding.

As families grow or your responsibilities grow after maternity leave, establishing a reliable routine becomes such a blessing for babies and parents alike. You can better schedule visits from others while the baby is awake. You can plan trips to the store and what you need while venturing out during the day. With this routine, you are setting up a larger, far more important concept for them. They are learning you are trustworthy and will provide them with reliable stability. You will take care of their needs and their voice matters. Both things help stimulate brain development at the optimal rate during these early months in life.

Setting up good boundaries around bedtime serves you well too. As a first time mom, the desire to rock Brooks to sleep was so strong. I felt like a horrible mom laying him down when he was settled and tired, but not yet asleep. I wanted to soak up all the snuggles I could. But, I knew we were on a path to have lots of kids and I needed them each to be able to self-soothe or bedtime would take over our lives in the very near future. Having a consistent bedtime routine of baths, brushing teeth, reading a couple books, and getting in bed took time, but saved hours in the future as they learned how to wind down their days.

Now, when a child wakes up in the middle of the night, I know something is wrong. Either they don't feel well, have a nose bleed, or had a bad dream. The first two warrant my role as nurse-mom to jump into action, which I excel in. When a bad dream happens, many times my husband steps in. Chris is quick to pray with them and asks the kids to list out their favorite things—favorite foods, favorite places to go, favorite day of their life. He encourages them to think through every time they've eaten those foods, places they've been, or details of the special day. As their minds meditate on those fun memories, it settles them back to sleep.

From a young age, our childrens' bedrooms quickly became a place they looked forward to resting. Being a family of eight, all of our kids have naturally shared bedrooms for a portion, if not all, of their lives. We also protect their beds as sanctuaries of refuge for each of them. They aren't asked to share the pillows, blankets, and stuffies in them. We also protect the bedrooms as a place for rest and don't use them as a location for time out. If we want them to look forward to going to their bedrooms at night, then we felt it would be best not to force them to retreat in isolation to their rooms in times of heightened emotional state. Now, for some children, the need to isolate for the safety of others in the home is really the best option, but for us, using a chair in the dining room has served us well as a space for calming down and having conversations together.

Through all the ups and downs of parenting, I want our kids to know they can rely on us to be there to support them in times of defeat, cheer them on through life's victories, catch them when they fall, and hold them when they cry. As my understanding of this unwavering truth in mothering my own children has grown, my depth of believing the same truth in the Lord's love for me grows deeper still.

The Lord desires to give blessings on blessings to all of his children. In the parable of the prodigal son, found in Luke 15:11-32, Jesus shares a story of a father with two sons. One son, upon coming of age, asked for the inheritance from the father before his father's death. This disrespectful gesture communicated, "You're worth more to me dead than alive," yet his father gave his son the inheritance and off he went to town. He squandered all his money on the pleasures of the world. Only upon hitting rock bottom, as he shared food with the hogs from whose pen he was cleaning, did the son consider going back. The son decided, "even the animals at my father's house have life better than I do." With his tail between his legs he made the journey back home to beg for his father's forgiveness with a place as a helping hand on the estate. He didn't plan to ask for his previous place in the standing as a son and heir to the throne. He simply wanted the lowest spot in the servants' quarters.

While he was still off in the distance, the father saw the silhouette of his long lost son approaching from the horizon. The father threw off his outer coat and ran to embrace him. Both throwing off his coat and physically running balked at cultural norms, putting his place of honor in the eyes of his servants in jeopardy, but the father wasn't bothered in the least by the perceptions of others. His only care in the world was that his prodigal son had returned. He ordered for a fattened calf to be prepared for a feast and threw a party to celebrate his return.

Jesus told this story to show our Heavenly Father's open arms, ready to receive each of us when we electively run astray. The son in this story knew the implications of asking for his inheritance early. He knew the justified disapprovement his father could have regarding the manner in which he squandered away his inheritance on the things of this world. Yet, he courageously recognized his weak, helpless position in life and came home. Imagine his surprise when he saw his father running towards him. He knew immediately that his father was thankful for his return. Did he imagine party preparations being underway? Highly unlikely, but our Heavenly Father celebrates each time one of His prodigal children turns and heads back towards Him. He doesn't wait for us to wash the stench of the pigs slop off of us and get straightened up; He runs with open arms, throwing off His outer coat to reach us and give a full embrace.

Just as the Lord delights in our return, He sees us as the best of all creation. We are the cream of the crop, the crowning jewel in all creation. He desires to bless us. James 1:17-18 states, "Every good and perfect gift is from above, coming down from the Father of the heavenly lights, who does not change like shifting shadows. He chose to give us birth through the word of truth, that we might be a kind of firstfruits of all he created." May we approach our Father with the comfort in knowing He desires to bless His children through the Holy Spirit. Jesus explains the desire of His father, compares the desire to provide for our earthly children to how God views providing for us in Luke 11:11-13. "Which of you fathers, if your son asks for a fish, will give him a snake instead? Or if he asks for an egg, will give him a scorpion? If you then, though you are evil, know how to give good gifts to your children, how much more will your Father in heaven give the Holy Spirit to those who ask him!"

In planning our daily schedules and the schedules for our children, we can rest assured the Lord delights when we ask for the Holy Spirit's guidance throughout our day. Our quest to provide for our children pales in comparison to the way the Lord wants to provide blessings in their lives. Philippians 4:19 explains it this way: "And my God will meet all your needs according to the riches of His glory in Christ Jesus." The glory of Christ's life and death on the cross was being able to send the Holy Spirit in His place to be our counselor. May we gain confidence in these truths about how the Lord sees us, even in our dirty sinful state: the way He keeps his arms open, ready to welcome us back when we go astray, the way He desires to lavish us with good and perfect gifts, and the way He promises to provide all we need. Let's keep our eyes focused on staying reliable for our own children, beginning with intentional schedules, in the ways the Lord demonstrates time and time again in His reliability to us.

**➡ Jump to pages 214-218 in the
Full Hands, Full Life Activity Companion Guide
for this week's interactive prompts.**

Week 37: Career + Motherhood

Busyness is just one letter away from business. The American way of life glamorizes both— busyness and business. Stay busy. Make money. Strive for bigger and better. All these driving cultural norms create an unsettling struggle between career and motherhood.

My own mother held a high-level, corporate America job in one of the largest Fortune 500 technology companies in the 80's and 90's. Her success in a man's world was revered. In her business suit and kitty pumps, she caught my father's eye as he worked in an adjacent building for the same company. Beyond her stunning looks, he was drawn into her confidence and drive. She held this position and continued climbing the corporate ladder amidst having my sister and I up until a life altering accident.

After our family returned home from a horse show, where we sat in the blistering heat of August from dawn until dusk, my mother jumped on the scooter for a quick cool down ride around the neighborhood. Our six and a half acre farm was situated at the bottom of a hill at the end of a cul-de-sac, and was a respite away from the hustle and bustle of the capital city. Once my sister and I had the horses and tack unloaded from the trailer, we noticed she hadn't returned. About this time, the sounds of sirens filled the air. My father took off in the car in search of our mom before we had a chance to jump in. When he didn't come back quickly, I took off running up the hill, not stopping until my eyes met the army of flashing lights at the summit. Unable to break through the barricade of cops at the scene, I caught sight of the scooter laying in our neighbor's grass. Whether she was hit by a car coming around the blind corner or simply lost traction on gravel and went over, we will never know. In the Lord's kindness, my mother blacked out during the accident and still does not remember the details to this day, but she suffered severe injuries. Her broken clavicle, shattered lower portion of her arm and hand, broken jaw, and severe concussion landed her in the ICU for days. The injuries sustained led to debilitating migraines, making her eligible for medical disability leave from that point until retirement.

Despite this, my mom exemplified a fight for life unlike any I've ever seen. With her jaw wired shut, I saw her communicate her appreciation and love for us through her kind eyes. Without her sense of taste, she readily drank whatever concoctions of liquid substances we brought to nourish her. She battled through physical therapy sessions to regain the ability to rotate her wrist and retrain her dominant left hand to write and type. My Type A, driven mother, responsible for balancing all the family logistics completely lost her short-term memory. Normal tasks, once natural for her, became foreign, but she never missed an occupational therapy session and diligently learned coping mechanisms to regain vital skills in her life. Sticky notes and memory mind games became her new norm. She never gave up on herself, on us, or her faith.

When she found returning to work impossible, she devoted her time to volunteering around the community. Remembering the joy bedside visits from therapy pets in the hospital brought her, she sought out a path to get her rescue Australian Shepherd, Phoebe, pet therapy certified.

My mom and Phoebe started frequenting the local Ronald McDonald House which provided comfort, care, and support for families with children who were sick or critically ill. Visits to the families and workers in the RMDH led to uplifting stories around our dinner table. My mom and Phoebe established relationships with children involved in a literacy intervention program in Title 1 elementary schools around the city. When reading to an adult inhibited their confidence to read aloud, the children forgot their inhibitions and read in Phoebe's presence. Their partnership in volunteering impacted the local community in such a tangible way that Phoebe was presented the "2005 Animal Hall of Fame Service Award" by the North Carolina Veterinary Medical Association for Special Contribution to Society. My desire to make a difference in the local community grew from the example my mother set for me.

Proverbs, the book of the Bible whose purpose is widely known as a guide to applying divine wisdom to daily life and providing moral instruction, consists of thirty-one chapters. This book holds many passages on women, and seems fitting that the final chapter ends with the picture of a noble woman. Much like a preacher who wraps up in church by saying, "If you've heard nothing else, hear this final point," or a teacher who hints, "Pay special attention to this as you will see it on the test," Proverbs 31 depicts this woman; strong in character, holding great wisdom, many skills, and unwavering compassion for those around her. Contrary to cultural norms of the time, the Proverbs 31 wife of noble character " . . . considers a field and buys it; out of her earnings she plants a vineyard...She makes linen garments and sells them, and supplies the merchants with sashes . . . She watches over the affairs of her household and does not eat the bread of idleness . . ." This woman gets up while it is still dark, providing food for her family and portions for those helping her family. Her husband has full confidence in her as she brings him good, not harm, all the days of her life. What a woman! She exemplifies the balance between caring for her family in the typical motherly responsibilities while also exercising discernment in the workplace. With this in mind, I've walked through the internal struggle finding the balance between mother and employee. I'm a firm believer that staying home to care for, raise, and instruct children is a full-time job. I also see the benefits of working outside of the home. When I started my lifelong journey in motherhood, I too was climbing the corporate ladder with the typical 8:00-5:00 schedule. Yet my mom's departure from a career synonymous with her purpose in life, inspired me to hold my vocation with open hands. My mom found purpose beyond her career, so I held belief that I would too.

Over the decades, my job has morphed to working from home while homeschooling. My hours start early in the morning before the sun and end well into the night, but the majority of my hours in the day are carved out for homeschooling and heart development of our children. The Lord opened doors to job roles allowing me to work during crazy hours of the morning and night, and with flexibility to include my children in many ways throughout the day. Had I sought after this specific solution on my own accord, I'm not sure it would have come to fruition, but praying to the Lord about the longings of my heart, and praying for discernment on a healthy path for our family ultimately led us to this current space of togetherness.

When the big decisions in life come up, the Lord promises to make peace in your heart with the direction you are supposed to go. My faith in finances working out amidst huge vocational shifts must have grown from the graceful example my mom exemplified when injuries forced her departure from corporate America. I've found heavenly peace, even moving in a direction that is contrary to societal beliefs or my original plan for my life time and time again:

* Deciding to embark on my masters degree in business administration, against the guidance of my employer, led me to the open door into healthcare technology.
* Leaving the stress of the sales position I was in

ultimately led to a successful pregnancy with our first child, a journey that had been unsuccessful for months leading up to that point.
* Taking a 50% pay cut to teach at a local private school seemed like a reckless financial move, yet it helped me hone in on my joy of teaching.
* Deciding to launch a local mentor ministry part-time, while already holding a full-time position, jeopardized my ability to be with my family, but the time crunch experienced from working two positions together made gaining hours back with our kids through homeschooling make all the sense in the world.

An unexplainable peace in all of these situations made the contrary to society, life-altering decisions, far less daunting. Currently my motherhood-work-life balance rests in a space where my heart feels peace. I still hold this balance with open hands should the Lord call my roles to shift. I eagerly watch for the Lord to show up and provide the context for the decisions in His timing.

Maybe you feel the call to go back into the workforce and pressures around you are making you feel like you are avoiding your responsibilities as a mother. Perhaps you feel called to stay home and voices are saying you are being reckless in that decision or causing too much pressure on your partner to provide, or your current situation is forcing you to work a certain amount to make ends meet and you long to be home with your children. Remember, motherhood is a lifelong journey. In nearly two decades of parenting, my vocational path has been filled with unexpected turns and detours. Seek the Lord in these crossroads. Communicate the desire of your heart with Him, the author of your story. Ask for Him to provide synergy between your inner longings and your vocational state in life. In all, ask for His peace to guide you in the right steps towards His future plan for the life of you and your family.

Proverbs 31 ends with a sobering truth, "Charm is deceptive, and beauty is fleeting; but a woman who fears the Lord is to be praised" (Proverbs 31:30). If we rely on our charm and beauty to promote ourselves through life, we will fall short. Both are unreliable in the long run. But fearing the Lord, desiring to walk in His good, perfect, and pleasing path more than being pressured into a path by cultural norms, ultimately is worthy of being praised. May we look to the Lord for His guidance and peace on how to explore our God-given purpose in a God-honoring way through motherhood.

➡️ **Jump to pages 220-224 in the Full Hands, Full Life Activity Companion Guide for this week's interactive prompts.**

Week 38: Parenting Hacks - Veteran Toddler Tips & Tricks

When famous actors are asked about their inspiration, they list off Oscar-winning performances of fellow actors. Professional athletes detail stats of iconic players in their field who gave their dreams wings. People emulate people. We are no different.

In our adult life, contrary to popular belief, we remain pliable, moldable, and capable of a new chapter. As I began writing this book, the task at hand seemed too large to undertake. Even after the rough outline was nearly completed with topics for 39 of the 40 weeks, the process to move into writing the prose haunted me. One Sunday after soul stirring worship, I went up to the front to seek prayer with a pastor. Up until this point, only Chris and a few close friends knew about this writing journey, but in this moment of spiritual openness, I asked for prayer as a writing deadline approached. Joanne, knowing nothing about my book but plenty about my life immediately knew the weight I held on my shoulders. She had watched our family grow from two to eight and knew the plethora of vocational roles I held in our community. She was a soft landing space for me, which is what drew me to her. I knew she would not chastise me for starting something I felt deep down may be too much to complete. Instead she prayed with me, asking the Lord for extra energy, multiplication of my time, and pockets of solitude to devote to creating this message for others, but when the prayer was over, she asked me to schedule a time to meet with her. I'm embarrassed to admit the first thought which entered my mind was, "We just prayed for discernment in prioritizing my already crunched schedule and you're asking me to add another commitment to the list?" But, the Lord is so kind in the way He puts people in our lives, right when we need them most. The Holy Spirit prompts our heart for meaningful connections. Unbeknownst to me, Joanne is an author herself. She has written multiple books used in the world of academia to guide institutions toward relevance and sustainability. During our time together, Joanne put to words the feelings I couldn't express: the weight of the unfinished project that was on my mind when I woke up and kept me awake at night as I tried to sleep, the constant thoughts that flooded in sporadically throughout the day that had to be jotted down for fear of forgetting them when time for writing surfaced, and the craving for larger pockets of time to devote to writing alone as cut up bits of time seemed less fruitful.

From her own journey as an author, she shared something that resonated with me to my core. When managing the pressure to deliver on a large project that could not be rushed to completion, a mentor encouraged her to find a hobby. She shared the initial shock of someone asking her to add in another "to-do." But this was different. It was something she could realistically see through to completion in a short amount of time. Joanne started therapeutically completing puzzles. Each puzzle continued to build her inner belief in her ability to realize completion. Perhaps you too are a person who runs head first towards larger projects. Do you have any smaller projects running consecutively where you can enjoy the finished state amidst larger, long-term projects, such as drawing, DIY projects, reading, photography, or needlework?

Mothering Practicalities

At the time of my appointment with Joanne, I was copying the New Testament. I had been writing it in my quiet time with the Lord for three and half years and only two books of the New Testament were left–Colossians and Revelations. I prioritized this time and scheduled out how many more weeks it would take to finish that project. I gained steam towards the end, devouring the scripture in the mornings with a newfound hunger, and finished several weeks ahead of schedule. Joanne was right. Completing that project felt like a victory. Although completely unrelated to this book, it gave me confidence to keep writing, one week at a time. Joanne's belief in seeing the finish line on this book kept me writing on days I didn't feel I had any words left.

Parenting can feel like a never-ending, large scale project as well. Many long for the "out of diapers stage" or the "all in school" or the coveted "empty nester" years. Even after kids 'fly the coop', shouldn't we still desire to guide them well into adulthood? Choosing a spouse? Establishing a home? Raising children (our grandchildren!)? Motherhood is a lifelong work in progress. Though we have little control over the outputs, we possess the power to control every single one of our inputs.

The game of motherly input control gets tricky flying solo. Since these gems may help speed up your motherhood success journey, I'd love to share a few parenting hacks with you. Early on in motherhood, I realized my go-to when struggling in a season was finding a book about it. Reading how someone else found freedom, gained wisdom, and made strides towards overcoming whatever area in my life felt lacking, gave me hope. And, I prayed. I found my thoughts gravitated to chat with the Lord about the options but became frustrated when the answer back was either too faint to hear, or simply didn't come fast enough. However, I noticed others gravitating towards people. They desired to talk through the situation and chat through the options, but when they received advice from someone, they kept asking for the opinions of others. They wanted to make sure a consensus, or majority vote, existed. On reflection, I learned a healthy balance between these three is ultimately a recipe for success. Pray, read, and seek counsel.

Proverbs 13:10 encourages me to daily find this balance, "Pride leads to conflict; those who take advice are wise" (NLT).

Maintain a pliable heart posture, willing to take advice and grow beyond your own comfort zone. When my heart is hardened, any sort of advice feels like an attack. I am quick to feel my pride puff up and defend my honor. There have literally been books I've picked up, read two chapters of, and put them down because the content was too spot on for me to handle in that season. I wasn't ready to change. I sought justification for the very habits and shortcomings I needed to flee. Even when confronted with unsolicited advice, I've found if I search deep enough, with lots of prayer, I can find a little nugget of truth buried down in the pain. Being someone who leans naturally towards defense, I find success with choosing mentors and giving them the green light to speak into what they see in my life.

Finding someone who has navigated the waters of life well in parenting, relationships, profession, faith, or whatever area you are looking to grow is paramount. A mentor does not have to speak into every area of your life. You can have a mentor for each, but you want someone you look up to, with a proven track record of success. This person's willingness to authentically share their struggles and victories makes your trek towards success informed in ways they lacked.

Now, I'm by no means a solid mentor option for every area of life, but if you are looking for large-family home life hacks, I'm your girl! I trust that along the parenting journey, regardless of the size of your flock, you will find some helpful nuggets in the following tips. They've added order into chaos and reduced the stress from the mess in my home for years.

1) Color code your kitchen.

No, seriously. Assign each child their favorite color. Ikea has a dishwasher approved set of 6, BPA-free plastic cups, plates, and bowls that were a great solution for our family. They are the perfect size and bright, bold colors. As our family grew in size, the newest additions happened to love one of the remaining colors (only the Lord!). We've never assigned the kids seats at the table for meals, so having specified colors allowed me to quickly glance at the table and know who needed to come back to clean up their mess after meals.

Plus, for the decade where we were battling food allergies, this became a huge win to make sure the proper meal went to the correct kiddo.

2) Limit laundry.

Each kid gets a particular towel. I'm fine with it being a solid color, striped, or heck, a wildly designed beach towel. The only stipulation is that they have to be unique and recognizable. When I find a wet towel on the floor, I know whose it is. Each child also has specific hangers for their towels. Minimizing duplicates helps keep from having unnecessary loads of towels to launder while building responsibility and good hygiene habits for the children.

3) Sort by clothing type.

One of the first skills toddlers can do, even before communicating in sentences, is sort items. I've always organized their clothes by clothing type: pajamas, tops, bottoms, socks, dresses, etc. Each clothing type has its unique drawer or organizing box. By the time they are two, our kids can be given a stack of clothes and know exactly where they need to go. This gives them confidence in picking out outfits and dressing themselves at a young age.

4) Magic diaper change.

Perhaps you are through this phase, and if so, pass this tip along to a fellow moms of babies! Lay the new diaper under the baby's booty before you even unlatch the soiled diaper. Then as you are removing the dirty diaper, use the front wet portion of the diaper to make the first pass on the back soiled area. The diaper's strength and thickness effortlessly handles the heavy load. This saves wipes (and your hands)!

5) Pet safety.

Bring home a blanket from the hospital before the new baby arrives home will allow your pets to get familiar with the baby smell. When the baby comes home, make sure you have an animal-proof, safe sleeping space. Cats, in particular, enjoy a warm snuggle spot, and you don't want cats snuggling in the crib, inhibiting the infant's ability to breathe freely.

6) Potty Training.

Keep the rewards coming, but glamorize staying "clean and dry." We are currently in the potty training phase with Lila, now 27 months old. Each of our children have shown interest between two and two and a half. Arguably young, I've always elected to go along with them showing excitement instead of waiting for me to be ready. What I've found most successful is making sure the schedule is a little lighter, and we can stay at home for a few days straight. From the very first day, I ask them to check if they are clean and dry. When they are, they receive a reward like a Skittle or M&M. Even if we head to the potty and they aren't successful at using the potty, I reward them for staying "clean and dry." Worrying about not being able to go when prompted makes them anxious about going to the potty. Rewarding them staying "clean and dry" encourages the end result I want—a child who stays "clean and dry." We also make every effort to keep our voices calm when they say they need to go. Instead of jumping up and saying, "Go, go, go!" while shooing them wide-eyed towards the loo, we look at them and say, "Great! You can make it. Let's go," while briskly walking in that direction. When accidents happen, I try my hardest to watch my reaction. There is a balance between acknowledging the mistake while not shaming them. My response is to have them answer two questions, "Are you still clean and dry?" followed with "Where do you need to go pee pee or poo poo to stay clean and dry?" I then have them help me clean up the accident. If you are in the throes of potty training right now, hang in there! As my mother-in-law says, "They won't go to high school in diapers. So don't stress!"

Just like in potty training your first child, navigating uncharted territory can be unnerving. It can lead to messes, blunders, and frustration. In those moments, let's remember our Lord promises to be right with us. The same Spirit Isaiah describes resting on Jesus in this way has been sent to rest on us, the followers of Jesus:

"The Spirit of the LORD will rest on him—the Spirit of wisdom and of understanding, the Spirit of counsel and of might, the Spirit of the knowledge and fear of the LORD—"
Isaiah 11:2

No situation or task is too trivial to ask for the Holy Spirit to rest on you. Picture the comfort and security felt when wrapped in a heated, weighted blanket. Asking for wisdom and understanding, counsel and power, knowledge and fear of the Lord, become the weighted blanket, comfort requests while parenting. Without the Holy Spirit, we easily fall short in our actions and reactions, relying on our own strength in parenting. We fall victim to the distractions of the world around us. This rings true even with potty training. As my littles have gained confidence in their loo expertise, they typically request, "Can I pwease hab some pwivacy?" in their precious toddler voices. Of course, I grant said *pwivacy*, and promptly get sidetracked having a moment to get something checked off the to-do list (cue switching the laundry over). Then, more often than not, the little one doesn't actually announce when they are done from the bathroom, but instead comes running out with pants around their ankles proudly announcing their victorious act so the whole house can hear. As exciting as this is, I know there is a trail proving their victory in need of a clean up, but we are quick to forget the accidents that occurred three outfits ago in a three hour period and wholeheartedly celebrate successfully staying clean and dry in the moment.

Let's be more childlike in our parenting victories. Let's ask the Holy Spirit to enter in our daily interactions with wisdom, understanding, counsel, power, knowledge, and fear of the Lord. Then let's celebrate the transformation we experience in our actions and reactions each day.

➡️ **Jump to pages 226-230 in the Full Hands, Full Life Activity Companion Guide for this week's interactive prompts.**

Week 39: New Life Care

To be completely transparent, I struggled when naming this chapter. We are nearing the end of our journey together, just two weeks away from launching into our newly birthed life. Our interactions within our own minds and with others (especially our children) will be fragile, so I want to take a deep dive into how vitally fundamental the first two years of a child's life are in setting a child up for lifelong success in hopes that we can turn the spotlight onto our new way of life needing a similar level of care.

Safety and infant care items go hand and hand. In 2008, when I started on this motherhood journey, the common practice for creating a gift registry (before the day in age of Amazon wish lists and Buy, Buy, Baby registries) required walking the aisles of a megastore like Babies 'R Us. The store clerk, kindly handing you the scanning gun, also provided a list of recommended "must-have" baby items. This "short" list contained 21 pages printed front and back of the items labeled as necessities to care for your baby. Words like "Safety," "BPA free," "Organic," "SIDS device," and "Leak Proof" were all over the pages, pulling on my hormone flooded mind and momma-to-be heartstrings. The much anticipated trip strolling through the baby items ended up being so stressful for my indecisiveness that I gave Chris the scanner and told him to, "have at it!"

To be fair, I've learned over the last decade and a half of bringing home newborns that the "must-haves" for successful parenting are forever changing. A new fangled baby product that "I can't believe we grew children into toddlerhood without" inevitably hits the market, yet the Lord created babies in such a way that they don't require much. Aside from nourishment, weather appropriate clothing, diapers, wipes, an infant car seat, and safe sleeping locations, infants are as undemanding in tangible "things" as they come. They don't ask for name brand clothes or shoes. They don't ask for special drinks or dessert at dinner. They don't make a fuss when their diaper bag isn't as bougie as the next baby's in the nursery. Babies long for comfort, connection, and security.

According to neuroscience research, 80% of a child's brain development occurs in the first 1,000 days of life. During these three years, "the basic architecture of the brain is rapidly building itself based on the experiences the child has and what the brain has to think about. Is the baby fed when hungry? Comforted when upset? Engaged when alert?"[27]

"Serve and return interactions," as explained by The Center on the Developing Child at Harvard University, "shape brain architecture. When an infant or young child babbles, gestures, or cries, and an adult responds appropriately with eye contact, words, or a hug, neural connections are built and strengthened in the child's brain that support the development of communication and social skills. Much like a lively game of tennis, volleyball, or ping-pong, this back-and-forth is both fun and capacity-building. When caregivers are sensitive and responsive to a young child's signals and needs, they provide an environment rich in serve and return experiences."[28]

Studies have shown that neglecting these interactions during the first two years of life affects the growth and development of core areas of a child's brain. As Kristen Weir stated in her feature article in the American Psychological Association magazine entitled The Lasting Impact of Neglect, "The list of problems that stem from (early childhood) neglect reads like the index of the DSM (Diagnostic and Statistical Manual of Mental Disorders): poor impulse control, social withdrawal, problems with coping and regulating emotions, low self-esteem, pathological behaviors such as tics, tantrums, stealing and self-punishment, poor intellectual functioning and low academic achievement."[29]

After conducting my own research, I've settled into a place of peace knowing that the most important item I can give my young babies is love. Caring for them, providing for them, comforting them when they are hurt, focusing on the serve and return interactions, one hour at a time.

In one particular trip to Wal-mart, several years back, I earned ample opportunities to practice the serve and return game of motherhood. Walking into the mega grocery store, I got glances—well, really stares—from dozens of people. The local Wal-mart had just unloaded new family-friendly shopping carts with a child bench extender. It is the equivalent of an eighteen-wheeler shopping cart. Maneuvering around turns requires blind entries into lanes as you can't possibly see beyond all the children and the aisle caps.

On this particular trip, I brought not only my three children who were five and under, but also my newborn baby girl. I was thrilled. I was able to put the middle two in the bench seating area with five-point harnesses. Facing forward they could see everything that was happening, but weren't able to reach far enough out to grab things off the shelves. Brooks, now five years old, was a pro at holding on to the end of the shopping cart. His little arms had the strength to hold on for dear life as we hugged the corners and flew through our shopping trip. Infant Natalie slept peacefully in her carseat set strategically in the shopping cart's rear facing toddler section.

By the time we were ready to check out, I felt like I was in the running for "mother of the year." I never raised my voice, there were no tears from any of the four children, and the infant slept the entire time we were in the store, so naturally I decided we would liven up the end of our shopping experience in the self-checkout lane. The kids did such a great job helping me check out that we didn't even have to call a store clerk over for any items scanned twice by mistake!

After loading all the mobile kids back up on the cart, we headed towards the door—me beaming with pride expecting people to ask for autographs. That's precisely when my world got turned upside down. When we reached the threshold of the exterior door, the oversized kid cart wobbled in such a way that the infant car seat slid off the shopping cart exposing the bright orange Warning! sign clearly stating "Do NOT use your own personal infant carrier or car seat." I watched the car seat tumble upside down and skid to a stop on the sidewalk. After a long pause, my heart skipping several beats, I heard the horrific screams from underneath. My first instinct was relief. She was breathing, but as I turned over the carseat, I didn't know what her precious little face would look like. If concrete tears up toddler knees with ease, what would it do to delicate, newborn skin? To my utter surprise, the five point harness, in which she was still fastened from her ride to the store, kept her securely in place through the fall. Aside from being traumatized from the abrasive jolt from REM sleep, Natalie appeared as perfect as an angel.

I could not get her out of the harness fast enough. Brooks pushed the eighteen-wheeler cart to our car as I calmed her down through the parking lot. I knew someone had to have witnessed that happen and would be coming for me! What mother doesn't follow bright orange warning messages plastered all over the place?

To my knowledge, no one reported me to the authorities in Wal-mart, but I avoided the store for months just in case. However, when the curbside pick-up option became an option just two short years later, I wondered if the security camera footage of that day surfaced in the Wal-mart boardroom clearly making the case that, "Yes, mothers will opt in for online ordering!"

One of the most controversial topics that weighs on the nurturing mother's heart is providing a safe sleeping environment for babies. This topic has been one of importance for thousands of years. King Solomon, often referred to as the wisest (and wealthiest) man who ever lived, ruled over all of Israel 970-931 AD. He authored many of the books in the Old Testament. In 1 Kings, when given the opportunity to ask for anything from the Lord, he answered with, "...give your servant a discerning heart to govern your people and to distinguish between right and wrong."

We've previously talked about how, just like King Solomon, we can ask the Lord for wisdom and discernment in mothering. What I didn't share yet is the "Wise Ruling" as my Bible so titles this section after his prayer for wisdom is granted by the Lord. Two women, who happen to be prostitutes, live in the same room. One of them has a baby and on the third day after the baby was born the other woman has a baby. Both boys, born three days apart. During the night, the woman who gave birth second lay on her son and he passed away. So she got up in the middle of the night and switched their sons. They both came before King Solomon and argued about whose son was living and whose son had passed.

Read how the king ruled:

"The king said, 'This one says, 'My son is alive and your son is dead,' while that one says, 'No! Your son is dead and mine is alive.'"
Then the king said, "Bring me a sword."
So they brought a sword for the king.
He then gave an order.
"Cut the living child in two and give half to one and half to the other."

The woman whose son was alive was filled with compassion for her son and said to the king, "Please, my Lord, give her the living baby! Don't kill him!"

But the other said, "Neither I nor you shall have him. Cut him in two!"
Then the king gave his ruling: "Give the living baby to the first woman. Do not kill him; she is his mother."

When all Israel heard the verdict the king had given, they held the king in awe, because they saw that he had wisdom from God to administer justice."
1 Kings 3:23-28

Now I know this tragic story is tough to read, but it is a part of history deemed important enough to take up real estate in the Bible. When new titles or acronyms are created, such as the case with SIDS (Sudden Infant Death Syndrome), the attention of these names makes them feel new, but this ruling occurred thousands of years ago. The fragility and total dependence of healthy life on infants has never changed, nor will the attention you put into continuing this new healthy lifestyle for yourself in motherhood.

If you lay down these devotional books and smother out the work you have put forth, the new joy in motherhood you've been growing will be stifled before bearing fruit. Let's keep our sights on maintaining safe habits that keep our perspective on positive growth. Let's nurture our children with appropriate serve and return interactions. Let's help set our motherhood journey up to thrive alongside our children as they grow into adulthood.

➡ **Jump to pages 232-236 in the Full Hands, Full Life Activity Companion Guide for this week's interactive prompts.**

Week 40: Mirror Images

I have a confession to make. I saved my favorite topic for our final week together, and it's a doozy. Given your diligence along this journey, I know you are ready for it. So, buckle up, and let's dive in.

Fortunately, and unfortunately, kids become our mirror. They embody the good, bad, and the ugly. My fifth child, Lydia, won the prize for honing her acting skills the earliest in life. Gestures she made while talking at two, the way she twirled her hair by three, and her head-tilted, duck-lipped picture pose by four all brought a chuckle to my heart.

Not all of the mirror imaging embodied in our home brings a smile to my face. When I hear the way our children correct each other, it sounds eerily familiar. It causes me to take pause and consider the real possibility that I sound equally as dismissive and annoyed as I voice correction. They learned it somewhere. Being homeschooled, I can't blame it on a school setting! Yet, from the other side of the room, I'll hear the youngest one, Lila, now two, taking phone calls from her dolls using my work greeting, "Hello, this is

Meredith!" with precisely the same enthusiastic inflection.

I'm thankful the Lord created our children to be our mirror images, but it is also tough to watch. Perhaps it is the toughest to correct! How can I correct one of my older children's tone in their voice without picking up on my own tone? How can I explain the importance of keeping their hands to themselves while I have my own hand gripping the arm of the child to gain their full attention? These heart check moments land deep.

My mother-in-law, affectionately called Mimi by her grandchildren, has a supernatural gift of putting into perspective the value of relationships over the value of things. She also loves holidays; Christmas, by far, is her favorite. She displays her collection of nativity scenes year round. At Christmas time, Mimi combs the Christmas tree lots all over town on a quest to find the biggest, fattest Christmas tree she can fit in her living room. Every year, the tree is adorned with tens of thousands of lights and hundreds of Christmas ornaments, and Mimi loves her tree holding as many Christmas balls of varying colors, textures, and designs as will fit. Each one is expertly placed by hand where it hangs freely without being constricted by other branches or ornaments.

Every year the tree is mesmerizing to behold, especially to little boys who instinctively throw all balls within sight. Chris and I introduced grandchildren into extended family vacations and holidays years before all of the other siblings. I remember all too well the first Christmas Brooks was old enough to walk. With his instinct in full swing that all balls were fair game for kicking and throwing, I knew the tree was a goner. When allured into the kitchen to enjoy Mimi's infamous toffee, we lost track of Brooks for one, quick minute before hearing the shattering of glass, followed by an "Uh - oh."

Mimi ran into the living room and I braced myself for her reaction. She kneeled down, meeting Brooks eye-to-eye, but instead of scolding him, she scooped him up in her arms and said, "Are you alright?" She inspected his hands and bare feet, looking for any sign of injury, and said, "Mimi should have known better than to put those breakable ornaments on the bottom!"

I expected backlash. I expected glaring eyes in my direction as if to say, "You've got to keep your eyes on him." Instead she exemplified putting relationships over things. Mortified, I apologized profusely for the broken ornament and without hesitation she responded, "Oh, it's just a thing! Ornaments can be replaced. There isn't an ornament on that tree that can't be broken." She meant every word of what she said, but what shocked me the most is that I knew she had ornaments from her late mother's collection that were invaluable to her. She had pointed them out to me during past holidays, yet her grandson's heart was more valuable than any past memory an ornament could hold.

As the grandchildren count has ticked up, the size of Mimi's Christmas tree continues to grow, but what makes it even more beautiful now is the way it is decorated. She invites her grandkids over to dress the tree. The lower third of the tree branches are so weighed down from ornaments they rest on the floor. The sparseness of the upper branches showcase the reach of her oldest grandchildren. The star of her Christmas tree is actually a crown of thorns helping us to remember the ultimate reason we celebrate the holiday— the birth of our Savior, Jesus, whose whole purpose in life was to die the death we deserve, yet through His obedience in death, granted us full access to God, our Creator and Heavenly Father.

Thankfully, my littles have picked up on Mimi's prioritization of relationships over things. When something breaks in our own home I hear our kids respond, "Oh, it's just a THING! Things can be replaced, but I'm glad you are ok." I am forever grateful for this mirrored trait.

Some of us come from "breakable" homes. Perhaps the breakable things weren't tangible items, but were relationships, trust, or moods. You walked on eggshells around certain family members in the formative years. Maybe you still do. If you look long enough in the mirror, maybe you will find that those in your care now walk on eggshells around you. Proverbs 22:6 gives us insight into the way we want to raise our children: "Train a child in the way he should go, and when he is old he will not turn from it" (NJKV).

At first glance, this verse speaks to raising a child up in the right way, with the right morals and standards, and teaching your children how to interact with others. It is true our children learn by simply being in your presence whether we feel like we are teaching them or not. Yet, this interpretation brings on a heavy weight of shame and guilt if a child goes wayward later in life. Upon thorough scrutiny, this verse makes a unique distinction. It urges us to train a child in the way he should go. This distinction frees us from boxing us in to training up our children to follow the path ourselves have followed. It does not state that we have to be perfect examples or our children will turn out to be little hot messes. If we help our children hone in on their spiritual gifts and individual capabilities the Lord has set out before them, then their paths should be unique from ours. This verse encourages us to walk alongside our children and help them discern where their next steps should be.

At the beginning of life, our footsteps are heavier than theirs. We help them clear the path, cut down the thistles, and forge their way through. We teach them about the perils of the forest, the poisonous berries, and plants to avoid. All along the way, we have past experiences to glean from and a higher vantage point from which to see. When we sense our path together has veered off course, we can help explain our thought process behind why and redirect. As they grow and mature, we start handing over the hatchet for clearing. We quiz them on the berries and foliage around. Their feet begin to be the first ones to navigate ahead.

If we exemplify loving relationships in our home, hold ourselves to a higher standard than that of the world, and counsel our children in making life decisions, then the Lord promises the image they will mirror will be reflective of the solid path He laid out for them before the beginning of time, and life path will be more closely aligned with His path for us as well.

My hope is that you continue to see your motherhood as a journey. You never fully arrive, but continually morph into a better, stronger, more equipped version of yourself. First, you are an image bearer and daughter of the Most High King. In a close second, you hold the position of raising up an image bearer of the Most High King. The beauty in a lifelong journey is that you continue in a direction without the pressure of reaching a certain place at a specified time.

When we see our Maker face to face, my prayer for all of us is that we hear Him speak the words, "Well done, my good and faithful servant" (Matthew 25:21a, NLT). He chose you for such a time as this. He hand picked you to love, care for, and guide your children for Him. Our children are only ours for a blip of eternity, but let's not lose sight of the impact daily walking alongside them in life can make.

Let us rise up into this calling with eyes eager to recognize the full life, John 10:10 version of motherhood that the Lord came to Earth to make possible to us on the toughest of days and the most rewarding of days. The Lord wouldn't want it for us any other way.

♥ Meredith

➡ **Jump to pages 238-242 in the Full Hands, Full Life Activity Companion Guide for the final week's interactive prompts.**

Notes. . .

1. Leonard Kniffel. "Reading for Life: Oprah Winfrey." *American Libraries*. americanlibrariesmagazine.org/2011/05/25/reading-for-life-oprah-winfrey/. 25 May 2011. Accessed 11 Aug 2024.

2. "Taylor Swift Live Webcast Read Every Day Lead a Better Life." YouTube, uploaded by tayswiftruclub, 22 Aug 2013, www.youtube.com/watch?v=mdgKhdcQrNw. Accessed 11 Aug 2024.

3. @iamcoriarnold. "I became a millionaire at age 41. I could have become a millionaire by age 34 if I had installed these 6 habits sooner." X, 22 Nov. 2022, 3:06 a.m., 7:38 a.m., x.com/iamcoriarnold/status/1595033921036902401

4. Twenge, Jean M. "Teens Today Spend More Time on Digital Media, Less Time Reading." *American Psychological Association*. 2018. www.apa.org/news/press/releases/2018/08/teenagers-read-book. Accessed 11 Aug 2024.

5. Gelles-Watnick, Risa and Andrew Perrin. "Who doesn't read books in America?" *Pew Research Center*. 21 Sep 2021. www.pewresearch.org/short-reads/2021/09/21/who-doesnt-read-books-in-america/ Accessed 11 Aug 2024.

6. Literacy Statistics." *Begin to Read*, https://www.begintoread.com/research/literacystatistics.html. Accessed 12 Aug 2024.

7. Aizer, Anne and Joseph J. Doyle, Jr. "Juvenile Incarceration, Human Capital and Future Crime: Evidence from Randomly-Assigned Judges." *National Bureau of Economic Research*. www.nber.org/papers/w19102. Accessed 12 May 2024.

8. "The Consequences of Dropping Out of High School: Joblessness and Jailing for High School Dropouts and the

High Cost for Taxpayers."*Northeastern University Library.* repository.library.northeastern.edu/files/neu:376322. Accessed 12 May 2024.

9. "The Relationship Between Incarceration and Low Literacy." *Literacy Mid-South.* www.literacymidsouth.org/news/the-relationship-between-incarceration-and-low-literacy#:~:text=According%20to%20the%20National%20Adult,work%20are%20the%20most%20prone. Accessed 11 May 2024.

10. "Hyperbaric Treatment More Effective than Medicines for Fibromyalgia Caused by Head Injury." Tel Aviv University, 25 Sept. 2014, english.tau.ac.il/hbot_fibromyalgia. Accessed 11 Aug 2024.

11. "Breathing Out the Weight of Depression - Louie Giglio." YouTube, uploaded by Passion City Church, 19 Feb 2023, www.youtube.com/watch?v=mkdzy9bWW3E.https://www.youtube.com/watch?v=AYwRqX6kSV0.

12. Berndt, Jodie. *Praying the Scriptures for Your Children.* Zondervan Books, 2020.

13. Fry, R. (2024, Aug 15). A growing share of U.S. husbands and wives are roughly the same age. Pew Research Center. https://www.pewresearch.org/short-reads/2024/08/15/a-growing-share-of-us-husbands-and-wives-are-roughly-the-same-age/#:~:text=On%20average%2C%20husbands%20and%20wives,and%20-4.9%20years%20in%201880.. Accessed 20 March 2025.

14. "Benefits of Physical Activity." U.S. Centers for Disease Control and Prevention, 24 Apr. 2024, www.cdc.gov/physical-activity-basics/benefits/index.html.

15. "Exercise During Pregnancy." The American College of Obstetricians and Gynecologists. March 2024. www.acog.org/womens-health/faqs/exercise-during-pregnancy. Accessed 10 May 2024.

16. "Covid-19 Pandemic Triggers 25% Increase in Prevalence of Anxiety and Depression Worldwide," World

Health Organization, accessed July 25, 2024, https://www.who.int/news/item/02-03-2022-covid-19-pandemic-triggers-25-increase-in-prevalence-of-anxiety-and-depression-worldwide.

17. Baker, Dan. What Happy People Know. Rodale Inc, 2003.

18. Ditton, Michael. "Free Goal Setting Worksheets." Goal Setting Basics, www.goalsettingbasics.com/free-goal-setting-worksheets.html. Accessed 11 Aug 2024.

19. DeHaan, Peter. "Seek Positive Influences." Pursuing Biblical Christianity, 21 Feb. 2021, www.peterdehaan.com/christianity/seek-positive-influences/#:~:text=You%20may%20have%20heard%20the%20thought%2Dprovoking%20quote%2C,people%20you%20spend%20the%20most%20time%20with. Accessed 14 Oct. 2014.

20. "Family History of Alcoholism: Are You at Risk?" *Los Angeles County Department of Mental Health.* https://dmh.lacounty.gov/our-services/employment-education/education/alcohol-abuse-faq/family-history/#:~:text=Many%20scientific%20studies%2C%20including%20research,population%20to%20develop%20alcohol%20problems. Accessed 3 May 2024.

21. Bevere, John. Bait of Satan. Charisma House, 2000.

22. Summerville, Amy, Ph.D. "Is Comparison Really the Thief of Joy? *Psychology Today.* 21 Mar. 2019. https://www.psychologytoday.com/us/blog/multiple-choice/201903/is-comparison-really-the-thief-joy. Accessed 21 March 2024.

23. "baby elephant syndrome." Segen's Medical Dictionary. 2011. Farlex, Inc. 12 Aug. 2024 https://medical-dictionary.thefreedictionary.com/baby+elephant+syndrome.

24. Walia, Dr. Belynder. "5 Tell-Tale Signs You Are Suffering From Baby Elephant Syndrome." *Brainz.*, www.brainzmagazine.com/post/5-tell-tale-signs-you-are-

suffering-from-baby-elephant-syndrome#:~:text=The%20Baby%20Elephant%20Syndrome%20was,become%20part%20of%20our%20identity. Accessed 12 Aug. 2024.

25. "Postpartum Depression." MayoClinic, 24 Nov. 2022, www.mayoclinic.org/diseases-conditions/postpartum-depression/symptoms-causes/syc-20376617. Accessed 12 Aug. 2024.

26. National Institute of Mental Health website, Postpartum Depression information booklet. Accessed August 2024. at https://www.nimh.nih.gov/health/publications/postpartum-depression-facts/postpartum-depression-brochure_146657.pdf

27. "First 1000 days." *ItascaProject*. itascaproject.org/first-1000-days/. Accessed 25 Aug 2024.

28. "Serve and Return." *Center on the Developing Child* Harvard University. developingchild.harvard.edu/science/key-concepts/serve-and-return/. Accessed 25 Aug 2024.

29. Weir, Kristen. "The lasting impact of neglect." *American Psychological Association*, June 2014, www.apa.org/monitor/2014/06/neglect. Accessed 25 Aug 2024.

Acknowledgements...

I have to start by thanking my awesome husband, Chris. From encouraging a God-sized dream to entertaining the kids for countless hours of solitude, he was as important to seeing this book through to the end as I was. Next, thank you to my courageous, honest, genuine and caring children. Through your untarnished view of the world I daily refresh my countless blessings amidst chaos. Through your forgiveness and empathy, I'm daily reminded of how grace looks and feels.

Special thanks to Megan for all the prayers, laughter and tears by my side, and for every unrushed phone call detailing God showing up again and again as the true author along my writing journey. Thanks to Joanne, Julie, and Kathryn - fellow authors who continued to inspire me to reach the finish line.

Thanks to Jess and Rose for giving pre-kid perspectives on essential topics to cover and the design aesthetic to strive for. I'm so encouraged by you—the next generation of mothers.

To my parents, Jerry and Vicki, a heartfelt thank you for always demonstrating your love and voicing how proud you were of my achievements—even through the undeniably rocky teenage years, for encouraging my independence, and for making church a part of my upbringing every step of the way.

To my in-laws, Paul and Cathy, thank you for taking me on as a daughter-in-love. Your lives as witnesses to the Gospel of grace will continue to live out through the legacy of Chris and I's parenting.

To Marie, for a heart-felt motherhood question which became the catalyst for this work.

Thank you to the United House Publishing team - Ashley and Amber for believing this message was pertinent to motherhood in the current cultural landscape, Jessica for heart-felt edit suggestions and keeping me on pace. United House Publishing for the spot-on cover design and Talitha for the beautifully intricate coloring pages. I felt the Lord moving through each of you along the journey.

Thank you to all the musicians who follow the Lord's calling on their lives to use their gifts and talents to speak His truths into the hearts of their fans.

And, finally thank you to every mother who holds this book, seeing value in growing personally to create fortified scaffolding of love for the children in your care. The world is a better place thanks to mothers who build deep roots of faith to share with their children.

About Meredith...

Meredith Juengel, mother of six, is passionate about leading mothers into experiencing the joy of motherhood in all stages. As a ministry leader, author, business owner and homeschool educator, Meredith writes from a full-plate perspective balancing the Lord's calling on her life outside the home, while staying true to His purpose for her within it. Dive into the beauty of her motherhood chaos to find celebrations worthy of tossing confetti within your own.

www.ingramcontent.com/pod-product-compliance
Lightning Source LLC
Chambersburg PA
CBHW070443090526
44586CB00046B/1661